RURAL AMERICA
IN THE INFORMATION AGE:

Telecommunications Policy for Rural Development

Edwin B. Parker
Heather E. Hudson
Don A. Dillman
Andrew D. Roscoe

A report prepared for
The Ford Foundation
and the Rural Economic Policy Program
of The Aspen Institute

Published by
The Aspen Institute
and
University Press of America

UNIVERSITY
PRESS OF
AMERICA

Copyright © 1989 by

The Aspen Institute

University Press of America®, Inc.

4720 Boston Way
Lanham, MD 20706

3 Henrietta Street
London WC2E 8LU England

British Cataloging in Publication Information Available

Co-published by arrangement with
The Aspen Institute

The Aspen Institute and its logo
are trademarks of The Aspen Institute.

ISBN 0–8191–7493–9 (alk. paper)
ISBN 0–8191–7494–7 (pbk.: alk. paper)

All University Press of America books are produced on acid-free paper.
The paper used in this publication meets the minimum requirements of American
National Standard for Information Sciences—Permanence of Paper for Printed Library
Materials, ANSI Z39.48–1984.   ∞

CONTENTS

TABLES AND FIGURES

v

EXECUTIVE SUMMARY

RURAL AMERICA IN THE INFORMATION AGE: TELECOMMUNICATIONS POLICY FOR RURAL DEVELOPMENT

Chapter One: Rural America in the Information Age

For nearly a decade, rural Americans have suffered one of the longest, most severe economic declines in several decades. If it is to survive economically in the 1990s, rural America needs new economic development strategies to grapple with stark new economic realities: the permanent decline of traditional rural industries, the growing importance of information-based services in all economic enterprises, and the untapped potential of new telecommunications services for rural business enterprises.

The structure of the U.S. economy is changing, with services now the most rapidly growing sector. This structural shift is mirrored in the rural economy, where public and private services now dwarf agriculture and manufacturing. Both urban and rural industries are being drawn more and more into the global economy. Yet the shift to services is only part of the change. Information-based activities account for the largest part of the growth in services, and other sectors are becoming increasingly information intensive.

The telecommunications environment has also changed dramatically. Technologies such as satellites, optical fiber, cellular radio and digital microwave have been introduced, and the convergence of computers and telecommunications has turned the telephone networks into information highways. But perhaps equally important, the telecommunications regulatory environment has also changed. The introduction of competition in equipment, value-added and long-distance services and the breakup of AT&T have resulted in new choices for consumers but also new challenges for rural policy.

Telecommunications can play a catalytic role in rural economic development. Unlike other rural development strategies that target specific industries or regions, enhanced telecommunications can help a broad array of industries in various rural regions. Just as in the past when a new highway or railroad link could boost the fortunes of remote towns, so today modern telecommunications services can help bolster and diversify the economic base of rural America.

Chapter Two: The New Economy of Rural America

Historically, rural economies have thrived because of location-specific advantages; they had the minerals or crops or timber which outside markets wanted. Increasingly, however, new economic development depends on specialized human resources, information processing and telecommunications.

The role of agriculture in rural employment has declined to the point that only nine percent of rural jobs are in agriculture, compared to 65 percent in services, 17 percent in manufacturing and nine percent in construction, mining and other sectors. In the past decade all increases in the number of jobs have been in services.

Few rural communities have diverse economies. Many are largely dependent on a single industry or single major employer. What rural economic growth has occurred in the 1980s has taken place primarily in counties adjacent to metropolitan areas and in counties with amenities to attract tourists or retirees.

The emerging telecommunications technologies can help rural areas better cope with the special problems of rural economies—geographic isolation and economic specialization. They are well-suited for the "post-agricultural" diversity of rural America, which is growing increasingly resistant to sector-specific remedies.

Chapter Three: Telecommunications and the Rural Economy

Investments in telecommunications yield myriad economic and social benefits to other industries, state and local government, and the public at large. They can faciliate greater price competition in various markets, eliminate middlemen suppliers, help lower inventory costs, facilitate timely delivery of perishable products, reduce the need for travel, and attract new industry.

Recent studies have demonstrated that investment in both business and residential telecommunications contributes to economic growth, with the greatest benefits occurring in the most remote areas. Much of the economic benefit occurs through indirect effects (called "externalities" by economists) that are not captured by telephone company charges. Therefore, additional government incentives may be essential to stimulate telecommunications investments needed for rural economic development.

Telecommunications and the information services made possible by telecommunications are becoming increasingly critical factors in agriculture and manufacturing, and particularly for service businesses. Telecommunications facilities provide essential infrastructure, like transportation and electrification, without which economic development is blocked. Nevertheless, telecommunications investment by itself does not guarantee economic growth. Development depends on the uses made of telecommunications services by rural businesses, residents and government agencies.

Chapter Four: Telecommunications Policy Issues Affecting Rural America

The 1980s have been a time of dramatic transition in U.S. telecommunications policy, as the FCC has steadily deregulated markets and encouraged greater competition. The breakup of AT&T has sent shock waves through the industry. Small rural telephone carriers, surviving on the fringes of the national telephone network, compare their plight to that of the last person in the children's game of "crack the whip"; policies that ripple past those in the middle of the market have exaggerated whiplash effects on those at the end.

Rural areas benefitted from the prior regulated monopoly through internal cross-subsidies that transferred some of the costs of rural service to urban subscribers. Now, telecommunications competition is creating pressure for every route and service to pay its own way. Without carefully planned transition policies, the longstanding policy goal of providing everyone with affordable POTS, "plain old telephone service," could be threatened, especially in rural areas.

Other regulatory initiatives may add costly new burdens and uncertain benefits to rural telephone users. These policies include price cap regulation, telecommunications ownership regulations, and open architecture standards. Rural America needs help in dealing with the side effects of policies crafted primarily for a competitive urban environment. Rural America also needs help to ensure that urban areas are not the only beneficiaries of the new telephone policies.

Chapter Five: A Portrait of the Telecommunications Infrastructure in Rural America Today

The long-standing policy goal of universal telephone service is nearing achievement. Most of the remaining unserved households in the U.S. lack service because of poverty rather than geographical location. For the remaining locations too distant to be served economically by conventional wireline telephone technology, radio and satellite technologies are now available to complete the mission. Assuming continued availability of Rural Electrification Administration financing, most of the remaining multiparty rural telephone services should be upgraded to single-line service by the mid-1990s.

At current rates of upgrade, it will be more than 25 years before rural telephone switches are upgraded to digital capability, which is needed to provide rural areas with services comparable to those already available in most urban areas. An increase of approximately 30 percent in REA lending authority for the next ten years may be sufficient to meet a goal of completing the upgrade of rural switches by the year 2000 and to make available additional rural telecommunications services. This estimate assumes that REA capital financing assistance is sufficient to help the smaller rural telephone companies and that the FCC provides regulatory incentives for the Bell operating companies and larger independent telephone companies to upgrade their facilities and service offerings.

Chapter Six: Policy Goals and Recommendations

Times have changed since those first telecommunications visionaries made their commitment to universal service, a goal that has nearly been achieved. Rural economies have undergone wrenching declines and the national and global economies have become more service-based and information-intensive. Amidst all this change, rural telecommunications policy has not kept pace.

It is clearly time to revisit and reformulate the goals for telecommunications policy. There are three primary reasons for government leadership in forging new rural telecommunications policies:

- To spur new economic development and efficiencies by helping provide a basic telecommunications infrastructure;
- To help rural America adjust to the new telecommunications marketplace by way of special transition policies; and
- To empower rural communities with opportunities to participate in the national economy comparable to opportunities available to urban communities.

Goals

A primary goal of an overall rural economic development policy should be:

Encourage rural telephone carriers to provide affordable access to telecommunications and information services comparable to those available in urban areas.

Specifically, federal and state policy should strive to:
1. Make voice telephone service available to everyone.
2. Make single-party access to the public switched telephone network available to everyone.
3. Improve the quality of telephone service sufficiently to allow rapid and reliable transmission of facsimile documents and data.
4. Provide rural telephone users with equal access to competitive long distance carriers.
5. Provide rural telephone users with local access to value-added data networks.
6. Provide 911 emergency service with automatic number identification in rural areas.
7. Expand mobile (cellular) telephone service.
8. Make available touch tone and custom calling services, including such services as three-way calling, call forwarding and call waiting.
9. Make voice messaging services available via local phone calls.
10. Help rural telephone carriers to provide the telecommunications and information services that become generally available in urban areas.

Recommendations

To achieve these goals, the following ten policy recommendations should be implemented:
1. Congress should update and expand the REA's mission to include fostering affordable rural access to the basic communications tools of the Information Age. Specifically, the REA should be mandated to provide loan funds and technical assistance to authorized rural carriers in order to make available to rural residents and businesses all of the telecommunications services that are generally available in urban areas.

2. Congress should increase the REA's lending authority by about 30 percent (approximately $150 million per year) to accelerate the conversion from analog to digital telephone switches in rural America and to help provide rural residents with access to voice, data, video and mobile services comparable to those available to urban residents.

3. The FCC should continue its support of rural telecommunications by maintaining nationwide long-distance average rate schedules. It should also continue to authorize "lifeline" and "universal service" funds out of interstate long-distance revenues. It should encourage the expansion of competitive long-distance services by permitting local exchange carriers to initiate upgrades to equal access facilities.

4. The FCC should encourage the development of video and other information services in rural areas by broadening the waiver of cable television and telephone cross-ownership restrictions in rural areas.

5. The FCC should offer incentives for the Bell operating companies and larger independent telephone companies to prepare and implement plans to upgrade completely their rural facilities by the year 2000 to provide their rural service areas with all telecommunications services generally available in urban service areas.

6. The Justice Department should recommend to Judge Harold Greene, in connection with the AT&T consent decree, that BOCs be given waivers or other incentives sufficient to induce them to provide infrastructure and gateways for information services in their rural areas comparable to those available in urban areas.

7. All federal agencies involved in rural development programs should include telecommunications planning and coordination and authorize funding for telecommunications services as part of their programs.

8. State PUCs should encourage telephone carriers to offer new information services by permitting accelerated cost recovery accounting on obsolete equipment not suitable for modern services.

9. State development and social service agencies should in-
    clude telecommunications issues within their planning
    agendas, and should request their PUC to remove any state
    regulations that inhibit deployment of new telecommunica-
    tions facilities appropriate for rural development.

10. State governments that have not already done so should
    establish a centralized telecommunications policy office to
    assist all state agencies in telecommunications planning and
    to help coordinate policy among various state agencies,
    including the PUC.

ACKNOWLEDGEMENTS

This report was prepared for the Rural Economic Policy Program of The Aspen Institute, under a grant from the Ford Foundation to the University of San Francisco. The Principal Investigator was Dr. Heather E. Hudson. Edwin B. Parker coordinated the report preparation.

The authors of the report and their affiliations are:

Edwin B. Parker, President, Parker Telecommunications, Gleneden Beach, Oregon (former President of Equatorial Communications Company and former Professor of Communication at Stanford University);

Heather E. Hudson, Director of the Telecommunications Management and Policy Program in the McLaren College of Business at the University of San Francisco;

Don A. Dillman, Director, Social and Economic Sciences Research Center, Washington State University;

Andrew D. Roscoe, Senior Consultant, Economic and Management Consultants International, Arlington, VA.

David Bollier, contributing editor, *CHANNELS* magazine, edited the report. He is also the author of Appendix 3.

Kenneth L. Deavers, Director, Agriculture and Rural Economy Division, Economics Research Service, U.S. Department of Agriculture, was particularly helpful in providing background information on the U.S. rural economy. Richard Adler of the Institute for the Future prepared excellent background materials which were very useful in this research.

The origin of this report was a conference on "The Importance of Communications and Information Systems to Rural Development in the United States" held in July 1988 in Aspen, Colorado. The conference was sponsored by The Aspen Institute

and supported by the Ford Foundation. The conference participants discussed numerous examples of the contribution of telecommunications to rural development, and identified several
issues they felt needed to be addressed by policymakers. A
report on this conference is included as Appendix 3.

The support of many people was important for the preparation of this report. In particular, Dr. Norman R. Collins, Director
of the Ford Foundation's Rural Poverty and Resources Program,
and Susan Sechler, Director of The Aspen Institute's Program
on Rural Economic Policy, provided support for the project.
Michael Rice, Director of The Aspen Institute's Program on
Communications and Society, moderated the Aspen Conference, and raised many key points which the authors have
attempted to examine. Wendy Cohen of The Aspen Institute
helped to turn the idea of the study into reality.

Mathew Schwarzman of the University of San Francisco was
responsible for word processing and numerous administrative
tasks required to produce the report. Tracy Huston of The Aspen
Institute coordinated the publication process.

ONE

RURAL AMERICA
IN THE INFORMATION AGE

1. Challenges and Opportunities

This report examines the results of changes in the U.S. rural economy and in the world of telecommunications that have previously been viewed in isolation. The structure of the U.S. economy is changing, with services now the most rapidly growing sector. This structural shift is mirrored in the rural economy, where public and private services now dwarf agriculture and manufacturing. Both urban and rural industries are being drawn more and more into the global economy.

Yet the shift to services is only part of the change. Information-based activities account for a large part of the growth in services, and other sectors are becoming increasingly information intensive. Manufacturers must now be able to respond rapidly to changes in demand; suppliers must be able to provide quick delivery for small orders; merchants must be able to update inventory and accounts records instantly. To stay internationally competitive, farmers also must resort to increased specialization and niche marketing, and react to shifts in consumer demand.

The telecommunications environment has also changed dramatically. Technologies such as satellites, optical fiber, cellular radio and digital microwave have been introduced, and the convergence of computers and telecommunications has turned

1

the telephone networks into information highways. But perhaps equally important, the telecommunications regulatory environment has also changed. The introduction of competition in equipment, value-added and long distance services and the breakup of AT&T have resulted in new choices for consumers but also new challenges for rural policy.

What is the relationship between these two clusters of change, and why should policymakers be concerned? Historically, rural development took place where there was geographic advantage in the form of arable land or natural resources. Increasingly, new economic development depends on human resources and telecommunications and information-processing infrastructure. In the provision of physical goods and services, rural areas could only compete across barriers of distance and geography if they had a natural resource advantage. In the provision of information goods and services, reliable telecommunications infrastructure can make geography and distance irrelevant.

If rural America is to share in the bounties of the telecommunications revolution; if its businesses and citizens are to enjoy equal opportunity to participate in the national economy; if rural economies are to retain some measure of self-determination as global markets become more integrated, then policymakers must take affirmative steps to help rural residents share in the promise of the Information Age.

However dimly perceived they may be at this point, rural America is caught up in these related economic transformations. This report seeks to explain how rural economies can survive and thrive in the Information Age rather than become victimized by it.

2. The Rural Economy

In the 1980s, rural Americans have suffered one of the longest, most severe economic declines in several decades. Despite some attempts to arrest this decline, government policies have not addressed the structural problems of rural economies with more imaginative, comprehensive approaches. If rural America is to survive economically in the 1990s, policymakers must begin to devise new economic development strategies to grapple with stark new economic realities: the permanent decline of traditional rural industries, the growing importance of information-based services in all economic enterprises, and the untapped potential of new telecommunications technologies for rural business enterprises.

The current rate of migration to cities from rural areas exceeds that of the 1950s and 1960s. There are fewer jobs in agriculture, manufacturing and natural resource extraction now than there were at the start of the decade. Just as in urban America, most new rural jobs are in services and more new jobs involve processing information than processing physical goods.

Rural America must adapt to increasing global competition. In both urban and rural areas economic success requires better information about national and foreign market demand and competition. Improved quality, lower cost and faster response to changes in markets are all necessary for survival as well as expansion. To improve productivity and market responsiveness requires ever more intensive and more efficient use of the tools of the Information Age: computers and telecommunications.

This report suggests the catalytic role that telecommunications can play in rural economic development. Unlike other rural development strategies that target specific industries or regions, enhanced telecommunications can help a broad array of industries in various rural regions. Just as a new highway or airport can boost the fortunes of remote towns, so telecommunications can help bolster and diversify the economic base of rural America. A more diversified economy, in turn, can help break the boom-and-bust cycles that typically cause great social dislocation in rural regions.

3. Why a Telecommunications-based Development Policy?

What makes telecommunications so attractive as a rural development strategy is its potential for promoting long-term growth, diversification and stability. Rural communities are not just losing their traditional industries; they are not attracting the more specialized entrepreneurial businesses that provide value-added services to niche markets. By investing in an enhanced telecommunications infrastructure that can serve the information-intensive needs of today's businesses, rural America can hitch its wagon to a rising star.

By contrast, development strategies aimed at traditional rural industries, while obviously important if only to mitigate human suffering, have less overall potential for reviving rural economies. Even if it were possible to contrive a wildly successful agricultural sector, it would do little for most of rural America. Jobs in agriculture account for only nine percent of all rural jobs and approximately one-quarter of all rural non-services jobs. The most vibrant segment in the American economy today is the service sector. Our economy's structural shift to services is not an urban phenomenon; it also affects the rural economy, where public and private services now dwarf agriculture and manufacturing. (See Chapter Two for more details.)

And so the economic decline in rural America persists. The number of jobs in traditional rural enterprises—agriculture, manufacturing and natural resource extraction—has plummeted over the past decade. The rate of rural migration to cities exceeds that of the 1950s and 1960s, possibly contributing to a number of urban social problems. There is an urgent need for more systematic, innovative approaches to rural economic development. Enhanced telecommunications, we believe, is one of the most promising instruments for a rural renaissance.

Why can telecommunications make such a difference? Most new rural jobs, as in urban regions, are in services. And most of these service jobs involve creating, processing, or managing information, not producing physical goods. Even those employers that manufacture goods or provide non-information services are using more information-processing services today than they did in 1980.

The growing reliance on computers and telecommunications is not hard to understand. These efficient tools of the Information Age enable businesses to improve productivity, improve quality, and respond more rapidly to changes in consumer demand. In highly competitive global markets, economic success is becoming more dependent on the skillful use of computers and telecommunications. Failure to adapt to this new economic reality means failure to compete and thrive.

In short, there is a growing economic chasm between rural America and the rest of the economy. The existence of this chasm is richly ironic, because sophisticated telecommunications can, as never before, overcome once-insuperable barriers of rural geography and distance. There is no inherent technical reason for the historic "rural penalty" of geographical remoteness. Yet the rural penalty persists because policies affecting telecommunications and economic development have not kept pace with the times and taken sufficient account of changing rural economic needs.

4. National Telecommunications Policy

The dramatic changes in U.S. telecommunications policy in the past decade have been, in part, a response to the pressures of this global economic imperative. The pace of technological change is accelerating, whether it be in faster and cheaper microprocessors and digital storage or in optical fiber, cellular radio and other transmission technologies. Because the potential applications of these new technologies venture into unknown territory, we need a vigorous competitive marketplace to explore the new opportunities. In computers, our competitive domestic marketplace has given us a lead over the rest of the world.

In telecommunications, the rise of new technologies in the late 1970s and early 1980s created two major quandaries for regulators of the U.S. telephone monopoly: 1) How could they stimulate new telecommunications applications and keep the U.S. competitive in global markets when neither the telephone industry nor the regulators knew whether any single approach was likely to succeed? 2) As computer and communications technologies converged, how could the traditional boundaries between regulated and unregulated activity be justified? While it was not politically feasible to extend telecommunications regulation to the computer industry, neither was it economically wise to stifle new telecommunications applications through regulation.

Regulators chose the only option they really had. They began to reverse the 50-year-old policy of regulating the telephone monopoly, ushering in a new, competitive telecommunications industry. The new regulatory regime and telecommunications marketplace has generated many important new products, services and cost reductions. For example, consumers now can choose among different types of equipment, value-added services (such as access to databases and electronic mail systems) and competing long-distance telephone carriers.

The regulators were aware that the transition to a dramatically different telecommunications industry structure would create many problems, particularly for rural areas. Nevertheless, they bet a major segment of the U.S. economy on their ability to mitigate the negative side effects of the transition and to achieve the economic benefits of a competitive industry at the completion of the transition.

Whatever the merits of those earlier regulatory decisions, it is now too late to turn back. For the sake of the entire economy and U.S. standard of living, we must now find a way to minimize the dangers of the transition and to make the new national telecommunications policy succeed in both urban and rural areas. (A "road map" to rural telecommunications is provided in Appendix 1 including the current structure of the rural telecommunications industry and the institutions involved.)

5. The Need for Government Leadership

There are three primary reasons for more active government leadership in rural telecommunications policy at this time:

(1) New rural economic development requires a reliable infrastructure of enhanced telecommunications.

Just as electrification and highways have played key roles in rural economic development in the past, so today rural America needs an improved telecommunications infrastructure. As mentioned above, economic success is increasingly linked to an enterprise's ability to use computers and telecommunications.

Investments in telecommunications have economic and social payoffs that accrue to other industries, state and local government, and the public at large. Unlike many business investments, telecommunications can generate far-reaching synergies for a local economy. Given a suitable telecommunications infrastructure, many rural regions could attract more private business investment. This upswell could, in turn, reduce the need for some social services that government must otherwise provide.

Current levels of investment in rural telecommunications, as decided by the private sector, do not therefore represent the last word on the merit of such investments. The success of such public works initiatives as rural electrification, universal telephone service and interstate highways illustrates how government can serve as a valuable catalyst for economic development. Government leadership to foster an improved rural telecommunications infrastructure could yield the same rich economic and social benefits as earlier rural initiatives. The amount of telecommunications infrastructure investment that would be made by the private sector without government incentives is substantially less than the amount that would be most efficient for economic development. Underinvestment in telecommunications will block the success of other private sector and government initiatives for rural economic and social development. Chapter Three summarizes the evidence and economic arguments for providing government incentives to stimulate increased private sector investment in rural telecommunications.

(2) Special transition policies are a fair way to help rural America adjust to the new telecommunications marketplace.

In times past, rural telephone carriers generally installed the same technology for phone lines (copper wires) as urban carriers, even though the longer distances involved in rural installations made this technology particularly expensive for rural areas. These investments in rural infrastructure were nonetheless made because they were subsidized by a portion of interurban long-distance telephone revenues, as dictated by regulatory policies of the time. The capital investment costs could be recovered over a span of 20 to 40 years. Now, there are lower cost alternate technologies for the more remote locations, including newly approved radio telephone systems.

Even though a new regulatory approach that encourages installation of newer, lower cost technologies has been adopted, rural Americans still must pay for the equipment installed before the recent technological advances and regulatory changes. Subsidies from interurban long-distance calls are declining, placing new cost burdens on maintaining the existing capital stock. To ease the burden of being caught between the old and new regulatory policies, special transition policies are needed for rural carriers. This issue is explored in Chapter Four.

> (3) Rural residents deserve an equal opportunity to participate in the national economy and determine their own destiny.

Many rural residents are fiercely independent. They do not seek government subsidy so much as equal opportunity to better themselves through their own initiatives. Telecommunications can play an instrumental role in providing equal opportunity. Enhanced telecommunications services can help rural residents to obtain access to expertise wherever it is available. "Tele-education" can deliver instruction in subjects that can not be offered locally. "Tele-medicine" enables rural health care providers to consult with distant specialists and to monitor patients from remote locations. Computerized databases provide agricultural information to farmers and extension agents.

These and other services, however, require high-quality (and in some cases, broadband) telecommunications networks, which are not universally available in rural areas. Given current trends, government leadership may be necessary to ensure that Americans can use the tools of the Information Age to overcome the disadvantages of distance and isolation.

6. Policy Recommendations

We believe that the government has a significant role to play in fostering rural economic development through telecommunications investments. It is inappropriate to recommend one or another technology in general; different locations will naturally have different requirements. What government can do is offer incentives to help rural telecommunications providers make available to their subscribers, services that will stimulate rural economic development. New government initiatives can help bridge the "telecommunications gap" between urban and rural America, spurring some measure of economic hope and ensuring basic standards of social equity.

Rather than make technology recommendations, we review the available evidence concerning which telecommunications services are most critical to rural economic development, and how best to provide incentives to the private sector of the economy to make those services available in the most cost-effective way they can. We conclude that one component of an overall rural development policy should be:

Encourage rural telephone carriers to provide rural residents and businesses with affordable access to telecommunications and information services comparable to those available in urban areas.

Without such comparability, rural areas will be severely disadvantaged as they try to compete in the increasingly interconnected national and global markets.

How much would it cost to upgrade the existing rural telecommunications infrastructure? Chapter Five looks at the current services available in rural areas and the rate at which they are being upgraded. By extrapolating from these newly collected and analyzed data, we estimate what levels of government support would be needed to bring rural telecommunications services up to the level currently available in urban areas by the year 2000.

We estimate that, along with certain changes in authorizing legislation, federal and state regulatory policies and rural development policies, achieving this goal will require an increase of approximately 30 percent, or $150 million, in the annual lending authority of the highly successful telephone programs of the Rural Electrification Administration.

A detailed discussion of policy goals and recommendations, including a list of ten specific recommendations for federal and state policy action, is found in Chapter Six.

To reap the benefits of the Information Age, rural America needs a modest but vital investment in telecommunications. Such an investment can remove a major barrier to rural economic development, stimulate more efficient private sector markets, and increase opportunities for rural residents to better their own lives. It is an investment that can yield huge economic and social returns over decades—if we have the vision to make that choice today.

≡ TWO

THE NEW ECONOMY
OF RURAL AMERICA

To appreciate the role that telecommunications can play in rural development, one must first understand the plight of the rural economy. Much of Rural America is caught in a wrenching transition; its traditional industries are declining, victims of new foreign competition, lower prices on world markets, and other factors. Reeling from such major structural changes, rural economies generally have not been able to take affirmative steps to develop alternate economic bases which might help them compete in the globally-integrated, services-dominated economy of the future.

This chapter examines the special characteristics of rural economies, how they have changed over the past 50 years, and how telecommunications could provide a valuable foundation for rebuilding beleaguered rural economies. In the following sections, "rural" is defined as those counties with fewer than 50,000 people living in towns or cities.

1. The New Rural Economy: Specialization and
Diversification

Mention the rural economy and it usually provokes images of farming. Such stereotypes probably have their origins from before World War II, when most rural citizens did in fact live and work on farms. But an array of postwar public policies and new farm technologies spawned an agricultural revolution, creating a surplus of farmers and a massive exodus from that sector. Between 1945 and 1970, an average of 120,000 farms was lost annually, causing an average yearly decline in the farm population of 600,000 people. More than 40 years later, we are left with fewer than one-third as many farmers, but farming remains primarily a family-owned and -operated business.

While agriculture still represents the biggest structural difference between rural and urban economies, farming employs only nine percent of all rural workers and only half as many workers as manufacturing. As Figure 1 shows, both farming and manufacturing are dwarfed by the private and public services sector; in this sense rural and urban economies are more alike than different (Brown and Deavers, 1988).

Figure 1   Services and Manufacturing Predominate

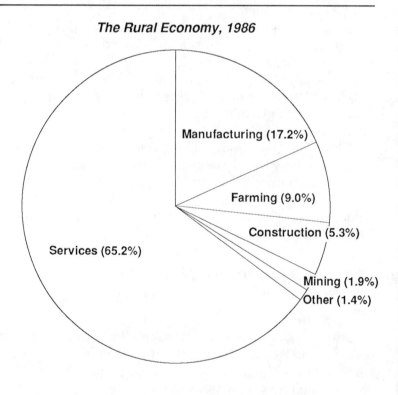

The Rural Economy, 1986

Manufacturing (17.2%)

Farming (9.0%)

Construction (5.3%)

Services (65.2%)

Mining (1.9%)

Other (1.4%)

All of the net growth in the U.S. economy since 1979 has occurred in the services sector. The pattern is very similar in urban and rural areas, with declines in goods-producing industry employment more than offset by growth in the services sector. Some two million service jobs have been created in rural regions since 1979, helping local economies which saw significant job losses in farming, mining and manufacturing. Rural services are dominated by wholesale and retail trade, other private services, and government (most significantly, local school systems).

Yet the rates at which this trend has occurred in rural and urban economies are quite different. Rural areas lost goods-producing jobs at more than twice the urban rate between 1979 and 1986, and their rate of service sector growth was only two-thirds that of urban areas. Thus even as rural economies become more dependent on services, they lag behind urban economies in their ability to exploit a national economic trend.

Farm consolidations following World War II improved the incomes of most families that remained in farming, and rural industrialization provided better jobs and higher incomes for many other rural workers. But most rural territories remain sparsely settled, with few towns of more than 10,000 people. Sequential specialization has been the chief process by which rural communities developed economically in the postwar era. Too small to diversify their economic bases, rural towns have moved from one economic specialty to another, as natural resource-based industries declined.

The overall result was greater diversity among rural areas, but continued dependence on a few major employers in a small number of closely related industries. The extent of economic specialization, and the different geographic patterns of specialization are clearly illustrated in the maps showing rural counties dependent on farming, mining and manufacturing (See Figures 2-4).

Despite the risks of "putting all the eggs in one basket," specialization seemed to be an asset for many rural areas in the 1970s. Mining and energy counties, for example, rode the wave of rising energy prices and oil embargoes, enjoying very rapid

Figure 2   Agriculture-Dependent Counties—Nonmetro U.S.

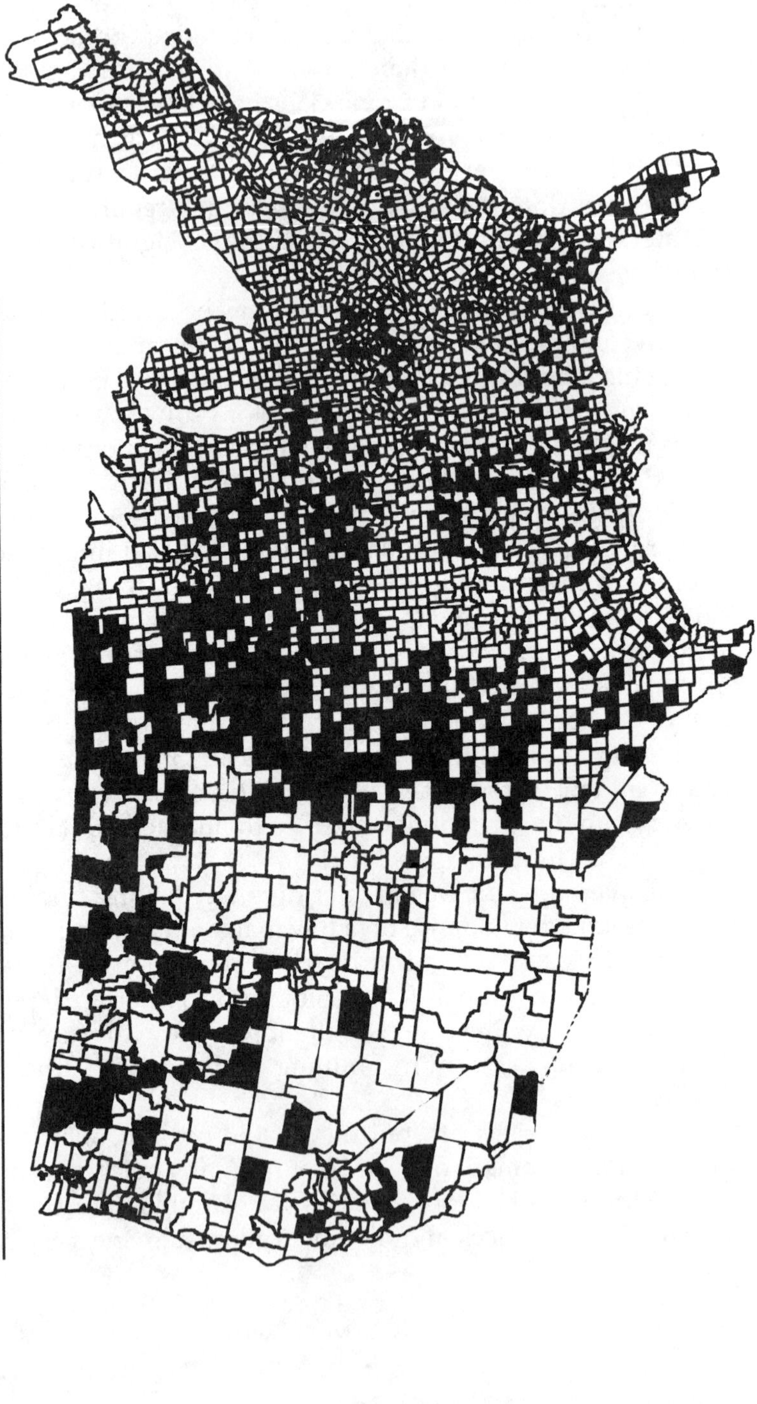

Figure 3   Mining-Dependent Counties—Nonmetro U.S.

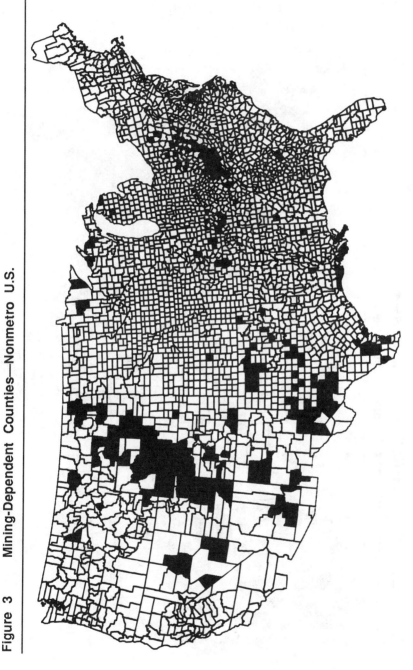

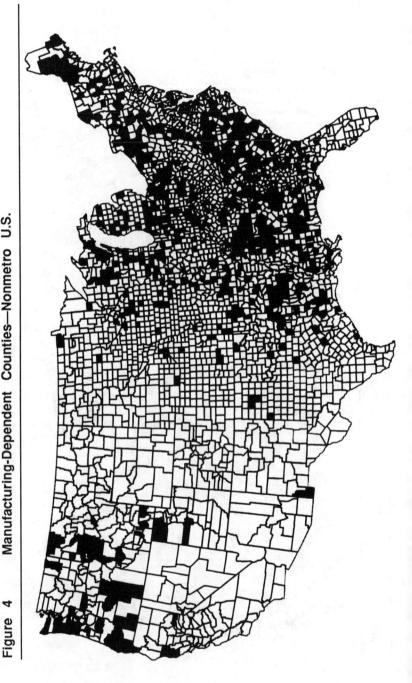

Figure 4   Manufacturing-Dependent Counties—Nonmetro U.S.

gains in employment and income. Other farming- and natural resource-dependent counties likewise benefitted from boom times within their respective sectors. Rural manufacturing counties, too, continued the momentum of strong growth which had begun in the mid-1960s.

Frenetic booms, of course, are all too often followed by miserable busts. This has been the tragic history of mining, forestry and agricultural counties. As we shall see in the next section, a wide range of external factors, not limited to national business cycles, now influence the growth and viability of rural communities.

2. Rural Economic Performance in the 1980s

Rural America's burst of superior economic performance in the 1970s ended at the dawn of the new decade, when the national economy began to sour. The national recessions in 1980 and 1982 produced a one percent decline in real Gross National Product (GNP) and a loss of two million manufacturing jobs. In the recovery that began in 1982, rural economies continued to lag behind metro areas in virtually every measure of performance.

Measured by employment change, the poor performance of the rural economy is particularly striking. While job growth merely slowed during recessions in urban areas, rural areas lost jobs, as Table 1 below shows. The metropolitan/rural gap in job creation has actually widened since the 1982 recovery. Only in the Northeast have rural economies kept pace with urban economies.

Table 1   Average Annual Change in Metro and Nonmetro Employment, by Region, Selected Periods, 1979-1986

Region	1979-1982 Metro	1979-1982 Nonmetro	1982-1986 Metro	1982-1986 Nonmetro
United States	.5	-.5	3.2	1.8
Northeast	.3	-.1	2.8	2.8
Midwest	-1.8	-1.5	2.7	1.5
South	2.2	-.1	3.5	1.7
West	1.1	0.0	3.7	1.9

Source: 1979-1986 change is computed from data provided by the Department of Commerce, Bureau of Economic Analysis.

The trauma for rural America has been especially intense in the 1980s because three of its leading economic sectors were contracting simultaneously. Despite large federal subsidies to farmers, agriculture counties have experienced severe job losses. As world energy prices tumbled in 1983 and after, counties dependent on mining have also experienced high rates of job loss and unemployment. Finally, the rural manufacturing sector was severely hurt by the 1980 and 1982 recessions, and has since made only a modest recovery. The magnitude of these employment changes can be seen in Table 2 below.

Table 2   Employment Change, by Sector, in Nonmetro Counties, 1979-1986

Employment Change	Absolute*	Percent
All industries**	1,330	+5.5
Farming	(333)	-12.9
Mining	(77)	-13.9
Construction	(10)	—
Manufacturing	(328)	-7.1
Services	2,010	+14.2

*   In thousands
** Includes additional sectors not shown in this table

Source: 1979-1986 change computed from data provided by the Department of Commerce, Bureau of Economic Analysis

Job loss in rural manufacturing counties bears special mention because those counties are much more populous on average; they contain nearly 40 percent of the rural population, compared to 13 percent in farming and mining counties combined. Thus the changes affecting rural manufacturing—the severe recessions, the downsizing of U.S. plants, the changing occupational mix, and the export of manufacturing jobs—have hurt more rural citizens than any other economic trend.

Not surprisingly, the rural unemployment rate has exceeded the urban rate throughout the decade. This has been true in virtually every year and every region, as Table 3 shows.

One striking trend that emerges from these data is the growing gap between rural and urban unemployment. At the beginning of the 1980s, the average rural unemployment rate was only seven percent higher than the urban rate. By 1987, it

Table 3   Unemployment Rates, Selected Years, 1979-87

County Aggregate	1979	1982	1984	1987
U.S. TOTAL	5.8	9.7	7.5	6.2
Metro	5.7	9.3	7.1	5.7
Nonmetro	6.1	11.1	9.1	7.9
Region				
Metro				
Northeast	6.5	8.8	6.7	4.4
Midwest	5.5	11.2	8.2	6.4
South	5.0	8.1	6.4	6.2
West	5.8	9.4	7.2	5.9
Nonmetro				
Northeast	7.0	10.5	8.1	5.4
Midwest	5.5	10.8	8.9	7.4
South	6.1	11.1	9.3	8.4
West	7.3	12.0	9.8	9.1
County Type				
Nonmetro				
Agriculture	5.5	9.6	8.7	7.8
Manufacturing	6.4	12.5	9.5	7.5
Mining	6.1	11.4	11.1	11.9
Retirement	6.6	11.3	9.0	7.6
Other	6.0	9.9	8.7	8.0

Source: Bureau of Labor Statistics county data

was 40 percent higher. Furthermore, this widening disparity has occurred even though the rate of growth in the rural labor force fell dramatically after the 1982 recession.

The recession of the early 1980s pushed up both urban and rural poverty rates. But since 1983, the urban poverty rate has moved downward; in 1987 it stood at 12.5 percent. By contrast, the rural poverty rate has remained persistently high; in 1987 it stood at 17 percent.

It is not surprising that the bleak economic picture in rural America has resulted in a significant exodus or out-migration of residents to urban areas, and a slower rate of rural population growth. From 1980 to 1987, rural population growth was slightly more than four percent, or about half the growth rate of urban areas. If current rates of population growth continue until 1990, the overall rural increase will be only about six percent for the

1980s, compared to more than 14 percent for the 1970s. In the Midwest, rural population has actually declined.

Furthermore, the pace of rural out-migration is increasing rapidly. The pace of net rural out-migration was slow in the early years of the 1980s because so much momentum had been built up in the "back to the land" reverse migration of the 1970s. Between 1980 and 1984, the total annual "outmovement" of rural residents was only about 30,000. Over the past few years, however, the rural exodus has grown to about 500,000 a year. This rate is substantially above the annual average for the 1950s and 1960s, which saw the massive postwar migration of rural residents from farms to cities.

3. Changing Rural Comparative Advantage

Historically, rural economies have thrived because of location-specific advantages; they held the minerals or crops or timber that outside markets wanted. In the early days of our nation the major continuing attraction of rural areas was the availability of cheap land to settlers. Through explicit public policy and the pressure of population growth in the cities of the East, people were drawn to the opportunities of the frontier. Despite boom and bust cycles as timber and rich veins of ore played out in location after location, and recurrent episodes of depression in farming, most of our rural citizens continued to make their living from natural resource-based activities. These industries had a major part to play in the overall economy as well. As late as 1940, farming, fishing, forestry and mining collectively accounted for 12 percent of the GNP and employed over 21 percent of the national workforce.

As long as technology and the composition of final demand allowed, rural America as a whole prospered. But after World War II, both these factors changed. Farm mechanization improved productivity dramatically, and millions of rural people left to take jobs in the cities' expanding factories and service businesses. This structural change in the nation's economy and the rural out-migration made many rural economies far less viable. Since 1950, 80 percent of the net new jobs created in the

U.S. have been in services. While many of these service jobs are closely linked to the goods-producing sector of the economy, they do not require a large component of "rural goods" such as food, wood products, and ores to produce their services. Thus, the growing importance of services in the overall economy has weakened the relative advantage of rural areas.

Only two kinds of rural areas have enjoyed strong growth during the economic restructuring of the 1980s: counties with "high-amenity" values and counties adjacent to metro areas.

Counties with high-amenity values often have lakes, mountains or shorelines suitable for recreation. Such counties typically attract tourists, elderly urbanites looking for retirement homes and proprietors of "footloose" industries with no location-specific needs except high-quality telecommunications and reliable transportation and utilities. Since 1983, 85 percent of the increase in rural population has occurred in the 500 counties shown in Figure 5.

These counties have a location-specific advantage because of their "rural resources" of natural beauty and low population density. High-amenity counties are likely to benefit from more retirees and rising incomes in the future.

Rural counties adjacent to metro areas have also grown rapidly during the 1980s. Between 1979 and 1987, their employment growth of nearly 22 percent exceeded even that of urban areas. Many of these counties are attractive sites for development as satellites of urban areas: accessible to the city yet blessed with the quality-of-life amenities of a less populous location.

Based on existing trends, the general rural natural resource advantage—farming, forestry, fisheries and mining—is unlikely to promote rural growth. In today's more integrated global economy, these industries have lost too many export and domestic markets to foreign competitors. Manufacturing, too, is a limited source of growth; American companies have turned increasingly to foreign locations rather than domestic rural areas for low-wage, low-skill manufacturing employees or to highly automated, less labor-intensive manufacturing processes. If future growth patterns in rural areas are propelled by

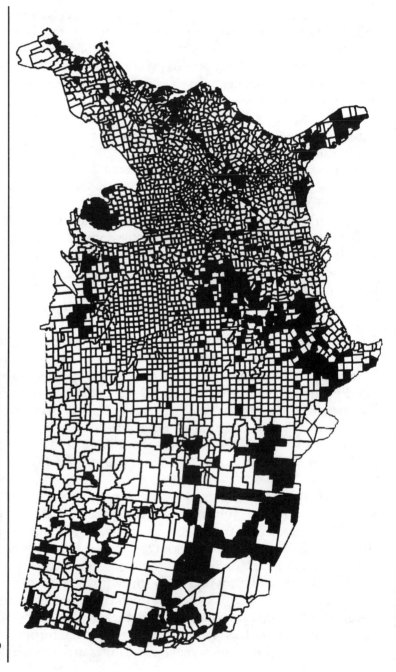

Figure 5   Retirement Counties—Nonmetro U.S.

amenity values and urban adjacency, the prospects for economic development in large sections of the Corn Belt and the Great Plains are all the more ominous.

The "postagricultural" diversity of rural economies means that sector-specific policies cannot cope with the breadth of adjustments facing rural America. Any successful policy must include a broad-based, comprehensive approach to dealing with rural disadvantage. The rural territory, with low population density, limited economies of scale, greater distance to markets, and more limited access to information, technology, and specialized services, will probably always lag behind in a purely market driven economy.

Yet the emerging telecommunications technologies can, with government leadership, help rural areas to reduce inherent disadvantages of scale and distance. Fortunately, telecommunications systems are highly versatile; they have useful applications in numerous business enterprises. This makes them well-suited for the "postagricultural" diversity of rural America, which is growing increasingly resistant to sector-specific remedies.

4. Human Resources

Any new strategies for rural economic development must address the quality of the rural workforce. Given the healthy growth in the services sector, many future jobs will be filled by information workers—people whose jobs are to create, process or manage information. These jobs represent new opportunities for the rural workforce, but they will also require the development of new skills. Young people entering the workforce must be well-educated, and older people must maintain or improve their skills.

How have rural communities kept pace with urban areas in educating tomorrow's workers? Both urban and rural areas have done a great deal to boost educational attainment over the past several decades. Between 1960 and 1980, the median education level nationwide increased from 11.1 to 12.6 years, while the rural median education level increased from 9.3 to 12.3. This apparent convergence of urban and rural education levels is somewhat misleading, however, because it obscures the difference in the populations completing high school and college. On average, urban areas graduate 10 percent more of their population from high school—70 percent versus 60 percent—than rural areas. This disparity has remained fairly constant since 1960, when the gap was about 40 percent versus 30 percent. Much of this educational gap can be attributed to rural/urban disparities in the southeastern United States. Rural America's percent of college graduates also lags behind urban America, but this gap is narrowing slightly.

The age compositions of rural and urban counties are similar. However, there is a striking diversity within the rural portion of the U.S. as suggested by the retirement counties map (Figure 5). Overall, the median age of people in rural counties in 1980 was 30.1 versus 30.0 for urban counties.

The similarity in age distributions and improved educational status of rural and urban America suggest that parallel efforts are needed in both places to improve the human capital available for development efforts. As lifelong learning is increasingly seen as a means of making available a quality workforce, finding methods for achieving that goal in rural America is particularly important.

5. The "Rural Penalty" and Telecommunications

In the section above, we have described the 1980s as a time when a decades-long process of urban growth and rural population stagnation or decline has reoccurred, accompanied by higher unemployment, a continuation of lower educational achievement, and other indicators that suggest rural Americans are not doing well compared to their urban counterparts. Any attempts to achieve rural development must take these factors into account.

Given this context, how can telecommunications help achieve certain rural development goals? It is useful to consider this question, first, in the context of existing rural development programs. There are four fundamental policy approaches:

- Sectoral policy targets specific industries for development. Most previous rural development efforts have focused on the agricultural sector.
- Territorial policy targets specific geographic regions for development, as exemplified by the Appalachian Regional Commission and the Tennessee Valley Authority. Territorial policy is receiving increasing attention as state and local governments assume greater responsibility for economic development.
- Human resource policy targets rural residents to help them improve their skills, stay in school, or relocate to other places where they will be better able to earn a living.
- Macro-economic policy, for example, nationwide tax policies, recognizes that rural America's economy is integrated with the national and global economies. National policies, though not targeted at rural people in particular, may have profound effects on rural development.

These four approaches to rural development policy are not mutually exclusive; nor is one "better" than another. They do provide an important conceptual context for understanding how telecommunications may contribute to rural development. The availability of appropriate telecommunications infrastructure and services is necessary for the success of each of these four general approaches.

By definition, rural means located outside of, and frequently away from, large cities. From one perspective, rural is all the residual space that separates cities from one another. Rural people live in small collectivities that are less densely populated than cities. Distance represents time, in an increasingly time-conscious world. There is little doubt that time considerations are becoming increasingly important to all types of business activity, as evidenced by the recent rise in overnight delivery services and the more recent dramatic increase in facsimile communication.

In a manufacturing environment that increasingly depends upon out-sourcing of component parts and just-in-time delivery to assembly plants, the farther a rural community is located from a metropolitan area, the more some other economic characteristic (for example, lower wages) must compensate for the time/distance problem. In an economy that depended greatly upon the extraction of resources (lumber and minerals) and farming of agricultural land, which were mostly located in rural areas, the rural penalty was a necessary consequence of being rural. In today's service-oriented economy, which increasingly depends upon information as a resource (or input) to produce a product which in itself may simply be a repackaging of information into a form with greater value, there is no inherent reason why a consumer or business must pay a distance penalty. In a resource-intensive economy, rural communities existed because means of resource extraction and utilization had to be brought to where the resources were located. In a service economy, that reason for the existence of rural communities no longer exists. However, if means are available for overcoming the problem of rural distance, then whether rural communities continue to exist can be decided on other grounds, for example, residential preferences and quality of life considerations.

A second aspect of the rural penalty is the economic specialization of rural communities. Typically rural communities lack the diversification that large size makes plausible. Few communities have an even balance of farming, manufacturing, or government installations. An approach to rural development that focuses on only one industry, one type of quality of life deficit, or one type of employment problem (such as underemployment), would in fact leave most of rural America untouched. We are beyond the time when, for example, assistance to agriculture could be considered synonymous with assistance to rural people. Thus, from the standpoint of how telecommunications policy can influence rural development opportunities, it is important to identify the telecommunications dependencies of many types of industries, from agriculture to services, and multiple quality of life concerns, from medical care to education.

The problems that constitute the rural penalty can be usefully distinguished from the kinds of rural development concerns associated with specific sectors of the economy, or specific quality of life concerns. One of the striking characteristics of telecommunications is that it makes possible a direct attack on these defining characteristics of the rural penalty. Computer modems and facsimile machines place rural businesses no further in time from a supplier or product distributor than any urban business. Indeed, the internationalization of economic production is predicated on overcoming the problem of distance. Overnight delivery which is guided by two-way radio, cellular telephones, and computer management systems places delivery times within the time frames of daily production cycles.

As Harlan Cleveland (1985) has noted, telecommunications offers a new means for overcoming distance:

> *The passing of remoteness is one of the great unheralded macro-trends of our extraordinary time.... Distant farmsteads can be connected to the central cortex of their commodity exchanges, political authorities, and global markets. The fusion of rapid microprocessing and global telecommunications presents nearly all of us with the choice between relevance and remoteness.*

Whether the promise described by Cleveland is realized for rural America depends on developing an adequate telecommunications infrastructure. Without such capabilities, the residents of America's more than 2,000 rural counties will find it more difficult to survive economically, let alone to prosper.

THREE

TELECOMMUNICATIONS AND THE RURAL ECONOMY

At the turn of the century, there was much speculation about the impact of telephones on rural life. One hypothesis was that telephones would improve the quality of rural life—by helping to overcome isolation and loneliness, as well as providing a lifeline in emergencies. There were many stories of lives saved when the phone was used to summon assistance for victims of accidents, fires, and storms. And the role of the party line in reinforcing the sense of community of those on the line was legendary (see Pool, 1984; Fischer, 1987).

Today, rural telephones still provide the basic functions of emergency assistance and community contact. Yet there are many other benefits, economic as well as social, that derive from rural telephone use. While many of these are derived from voice communications ("plain old telephone service" or POTS), to an increasing degree, the ability to send and receive data in the form of prices, weather forecasts, purchase orders, or reports is enhancing rural productivity. Telecommunications should now be considered vital infrastructure for rural development, a complement to other development investments that can improve productivity and efficiency of rural agriculture, industry, and social services, and can enhance the quality of life in rural regions.

The purpose of this chapter is to provide a brief summary of the state of our knowledge about the role of telecommunications in the rural development process. The first part of the chapter summarizes what we have learned about the role of telecommunications in economic development from research conducted both in the United States and in other countries. The second part examines how telecommunications contributes to development of particular rural activities in the United States.

How do telecommunications technologies contribute to the rural development process? Access to information is key to a wide range of rural activities including agriculture, manufacturing, transportation, education, health care and social services. Instantaneous communication can help improve *efficiency*, or the ratio of output to cost; *effectiveness*, or the quality of products and services; and *equity*, or the distribution of benefits throughout the society (Hudson, 1984).

Research over the past decade has shed considerable light on how telecommunications contributes to economic development. While more research may be needed to refine our knowledge, several conclusions can be confidently stated:

(1) Investment in telecommunications contributes to economic growth.

(2) Both residential and business telephones contribute to economic growth.

(3) The indirect benefits of telecommunications generally greatly exceed the revenues generated by the telecommunications network.

(4) Rural and remote areas where distances are greater and telephone penetration is generally lower may benefit most from telecommunications investment.

(5) Telecommunications acts as a complement in the rural development process; that is, other conditions must also exist for telecommunications to yield maximum development benefits.

(6) Use of telecommunications can improve the quality and accessibility of education, health care and other social services.

(7) Telecommunications can help a wide range of rural businesses and organizations improve productivity,

boost product quality, provide more efficient services, and reduce costs.

(8) Telecommunications can foster a sense of community and strengthen cultural identity, which contribute to development in intangible but important ways.

The following sections elaborate on the research which supports these conclusions and illustrate how telecommunications can contribute to development.

1. Telecommunications and Economic Growth

Numerous studies have demonstrated a strong positive correlation between per capita investment in telecommunications and economic development measured by GNP (Gross National Product) per capita or a similar measure. However, this simple correlation did not explain what appears to be a chicken and egg relationship—does investment in telecommunications contribute to economic growth, or does economic growth lead to investment in telecommunications? Studies on the role of telecommunications are generally of two types: case studies that examine the impact of telecommunications use in a particular sector or industry (such as farming, manufacturing, retailing, shipping) and macro-level studies that attempt to investigate the role of telecommunications in the economy as a whole. The latter are very complex to undertake, partly because of the difficulty in obtaining and disaggregating reliable data, and more importantly because of the difficulty in developing a methodology that controls for all of the other changes in the economy, such as investments in other sectors, changing market conditions, and demographic shifts.

The quandary was resolved, in part, by a pioneering macro-level study conducted by Hardy (1980). As expected, Hardy found that economic development leads to greater investment in telecommunications; in thriving economies, demand increases and more funds are available to extend telephone services. But Hardy's more significant finding was that investment in telecommunications does indeed also contribute to economic development, as measured by Gross Domestic Product (GDP). He also found that both residential and business telephones lead to increased economic development. And the economic impact of improved telecommunications is comparatively greater in regions with low telephone density (or number of telephones per hundred population), which are generally rural and remote areas.

Using Hardy's model, Parker (1983) calculated the indirect benefits of the U.S. Rural Electrification Administration's (REA) telephone loan program, which has helped rural telephone companies and cooperatives to provide telephone service to approximately three million subscribers. Parker estimated that the use of telephones financed by the REA contributed $283 million to the U.S. GDP in 1980. In addition, the government reaped new tax revenues of $196 million from REA borrowers and additional tax revenues from subscribers whose income had increased as a result of telephone use. Parker estimated that the likely benefits to the U.S. economy—as measured by expanded GDP attributable to the REA telephone loan program—are between six and seven times greater than the government's loan subsidies.

2. Indirect Benefits of Telecommunications Investment

The indirect benefits of telecommunications are related to the function of conveying information. Information is critical for rural development activities including administration and management, trade, and consultation. Information has some unusual economic properties that help explain why telecommunications can yield such impressive economic returns on investment.

First, unlike physical goods, information can be sold without the seller giving up possession. Second, the benefits of information may extend well beyond those parties directly involved in an information transaction. For example, if an agricultural extension agent can contact an agronomist to find out how to eliminate a crop fungus, the information can benefit many farmers. If a general practitioner in a rural clinic can consult with specialists at major medical centers, the chief beneficiaries are rural patients.

But even more important in terms of development is the fact that the society as a whole will benefit from these uses of telecommunications, both in economic terms and in improved quality of life.

Among the benefits of telecommunications for improving efficiency and productivity are the following:

Price information: Producers such as farmers and fishermen can compare prices in various markets, allowing them to get the highest prices for their produce, eliminate local middlemen, and to modify the mix and volume of their products in response to market demand.

Reduction of downtime: Timely ordering of spare parts and immediate contact with technicians and service personnel can reduce time lost due to broken machinery.

Reduction of inventory: Businesses can reduce their inventories and save money if replacements can be ordered and delivered as needed.

Timely delivery of products to market: If producers and shippers can better coordinate delivery of products to market, they can reduce spoilage, improve processing efficiency, and obtain higher prices for produce.

Reduced travel costs: In some circumstances telecommunications may be substituted for travel, resulting in significant savings in personnel time and travel costs.

Energy savings: Telecommunications can be used to plan trips, avoid unnecessary travel, and minimize fuel consumption.

Decentralization: Good telecommunications can help to attract businesses to rural areas and decentralize economic activities.

The indirect benefits of telecommunications for rural businesses and social services have been documented by several studies sponsored by the International Telecommunication Union (see, for example, Pierce and Jequier, 1983; ITU, 1986, 1988a, 1988b, 1988c), and the World Bank (Saunders, Warford and Wellenius, 1983), and by other development agencies. These and other studies show that the measurable benefits of telecommunications use exceed their costs (that is, revenues to telephone companies) by many times. Ratios of benefits to costs range from 5 to 1 to more than 100 to 1, based on improved efficiency in managing rural enterprises, time savings in ordering spare parts, and savings in travel costs and time.

Three important conclusions can be derived from research on the indirect benefits of telecommunications:

(1) There is likely to be a surplus of benefits over costs to the customers of a telecommunications system.

(2) These benefits may accrue to both parties in the transaction as well as to interested third parties and society at large.

(3) Revenues of telephone companies from calls generally do not reflect the indirect economic benefits derived, which are likely to be much greater.

Telephone companies understandably do not tend to take indirect benefits into account when deciding how much to invest in telecommunications and where and when to upgrade facilities; as prudent business people they must base such decisions exclusively on their own anticipated revenues. But in light of the enormous stream of indirect benefits, telecommunications networks should be considered part of a community's basic infrastructure, along with roads, water mains and electrical power grids, which are justified in part on the basis of their importance to economic development and quality of life.

3. Rural and Remote Areas Benefit Most from Telecommunications

People who live in rural and remote areas tend to grasp immediately the benefits of telecommunications. They know that the only other means of communicating quickly is through personal contact, which is likely to require a time-consuming and expensive trip. Not surprisingly, rural residents tend to use telecommunications more heavily and spend more of their disposable income on telephone calls than do city dwellers. In Alaska and northern Canada, native people spend more than three times as much as their urban counterparts on long-distance calls, even though their average income is generally lower than their urban peers. The only alternative means of getting a message through quickly is to take an expensive trip on a bush plane, since there are no roads in the remote north.

In these northern communities, growth in telephone use has increased so rapidly that telecommunications authorities have had to activate extra circuits in village satellite earth stations much sooner than anticipated. The number of long-distance calls in some Indian villages in northern Canada increased by as much as 800 percent after satellite earth stations replaced high frequency radios. In Alaska, the installation of small satellite earth stations in villages also sparked tremendous growth in telephone use. When local telephone exchanges were installed in some villages, long-distance telephone traffic spurted again by up to 350 percent (Hudson, 1984).

The economic benefits of telecommunications use are thus related to distance. The greater the distance from communities of interest, the greater the savings in travel costs and time. Similarly, benefits per telephone are likely to be greatest where telephone density is lowest. The greatest payoff from telecommunications investment, therefore, may be in rural and isolated areas.

For private telecommunications providers, of course, these areas simply do not generate as much total revenue as higher density areas, even with the higher revenue per telephone subscriber. This reality suggests two conclusions: special incentives may be necessary to upgrade telecommunications networks in rural and remote areas; and such facilities must be designed to keep capital, operating and maintenance costs as low as possible.

4. Telecommunications as a Complement in Rural Development

The research findings outlined above show that telecommunications can contribute significantly to socio-economic development. However, many other factors may influence whether and to what extent telecommunications may make an impact.

Generally, certain levels of other basic infrastructure as well as organizational activity are required for the indirect benefits of telecommunications to be realized. For example, a well managed decentralized organization such as a manufacturing enterprise, a tourist development, or a health service will derive more benefits from telecommunications than a poorly managed or understaffed operation. Telecommunications may also serve as a catalyst at certain stages of the rural development process, becoming particularly important when other innovations are introduced such as improved farming practices, lines of credit, incentives for decentralization and diversification of the rural economic base.

Rural development planners must keep in mind the context within which telecommunications will be used. For example, telecommunications alone cannot improve shipping efficiencies, reduce inventories and find the best markets for produce; a reliable transportation system is needed as well. A telecommunications link to an outside doctor or specialist will have limited value if there is no transportation to deliver special drugs or evacuate dangerously ill patients.

5. The Growing Rural Need for Enhanced Telecommunications

As U.S. rural economic activities and social services become more information intensive, they rely more heavily on access to high quality telecommunications facilities. Some businesses now simply cannot operate without these telecommunications links. For example, when a pharmaceutical wholesaler began requiring retailers to place orders via online computers rather than via mail or telephone, it put new pressures on rural pharmacies to install computer modems. Similarly, a machinery dealer was required by his manufacturer/distributor to install a direct computer connection at a cost of tens of thousands of dollars. Other rural businesses are finding they must have adequate voice, facsimile, and data links. Many education and health services are coming to rely on telecommunications to provide access to diverse, high-quality expertise in cities.

A new web of telecommunications dependencies is developing, altering the employment opportunities available in rural America and the routine ways in which rural businesses operate. These dependencies are also changing what services are available to rural people and the means and timeliness of their delivery. More striking, however, is the overall breadth of change now occurring in virtually all areas of business and social services, as is shown in the following sections.

Manufacturing

In an earlier era, the archetypal manufacturing plant was dedicated to mass production methods, received large orders from a few sources well in advance of the expected delivery time, made large production runs, and shipped products in large quantities to a few wholesalers. The product was sold mostly in the United States, supported by mass media marketing methods. The factory also had substantial warehouse space to support storage of component parts for needed production.

The manufacturing plant of the 1980s is more likely to receive smaller orders with demand for quick delivery, with penalties assessed for delivering too late or too early. Manufacturing equipment can be retooled quickly using computer software, often from remote locations, to accomplish small production runs. Component parts are as likely to come from a foreign country as from the U.S., and the products are nearly as likely to be shipped overseas as to be marketed domestically. Because manufacturers can electronically send detailed engineering specifications, including blueprints, to other companies, there is greater out-sourcing of component parts without a loss of quality control.

In this type of manufacturing environment, a rural business that cannot send or receive fax messages, including those sent computer to computer; that cannot receive software instructions for retooling equipment; or that cannot get daily access to requests for bids will find it very difficult to be competitive. Access to such telecommunications services is now as important as traditional access to good highways, water, and electricity.

Manufacturing has traditionally moved to rural America to escape high labor costs and expenses associated with urbanization. Such cost differences will continue to provide reasons for relocation, but only if rural businesses can remain effectively tethered through information technologies to other businesses. To remain competitive in our increasingly time-conscious, information-dependent society, manufacturing must be able to respond quickly to changing market demands and the need for small production runs and quick delivery.

Agriculture

Despite an overall decline in rural America's dependency on agriculture, farming is the economic mainstay for some 700 rural counties and an important sector in hundreds of other counties. U.S. agriculture earns $30 to $40 billion a year in exports, but world markets are growing increasingly competitive. American agriculture will have to undergo some major changes in the years ahead.

The image of America's farms is one of individual proprietors making their own decisions. In reality, production of many agricultural commodities, for example, wheat and corn, represents one of the last of our giant mass production industries. Because the agricultural production system is structured to produce the same product at a low cost, individual consumer preferences are for the most part ignored. Several factors have converged to encourage American farmers to produce crops in this manner. During the rise of the mass society, American farmers were encouraged to adopt the same high yielding varieties and to grow them in the same way. Standard recommendations from cooperative extension services and other information providers and the near singular emphasis on getting the highest possible yields also encouraged homogeneity.

In addition, the heritage of the community control era, when farmers looked to other farmers to see how their crop was doing, further encouraged similar means of production. The prevailing marketing system of this era resulted in each farmer's grain being dumped into community elevators and ultimately into community railroad boxcars and ocean barges. This system precluded differentiating one farmer's product from another's. As a result, there was no incentive for farmers to track their own products or receive specific consumer feedback. The little consumer feedback a farmer did receive was aimed at encouraging small changes in the standard product, and not at satisfying the different demands of various consumers. This mass production system is still the norm for some commodities, held in place by government subsidy programs that focus upon yield per acre and mass grading standards that fail to recognize the needs of market segments. It is hard to imagine a system better designed for a mass market or more inappropriate for an information age economy.

The only information that farmers once needed to run their businesses—weather forecasts and advice about when to plant and harvest—could be easily obtained from radio broadcasts. Increasingly, however, farmers use personal computers connected to telephone lines to obtain additional specialized information, including commodity price data and even weather forecasts for other countries, to help determine what crops to plant and in what quantities.

Like so many other industries, however, agriculture must become more responsive to changing consumer demand for more specialized products. The penalties of clinging to obsolete mass-production norms can be seen in the Pacific Northwest, where wheat growers continue to produce only a few wheat varieties, all of which are cultivated by standardized methods. (Some 50 varieties of wheat could be grown in this region, and different cultivation methods could produce further differentiation.) Pomeranz, Rubenthaler and Sullivan (1987) point out that the mass-production wheat-growing strategy leaves export-oriented agriculture highly vulnerable: "We [farmers] have been saying for many years that we know what is best for our customers and we have one wheat that meets all their needs. This is tantamount to saying that if they do not like our wheat, they can get it elsewhere. This is what they have done."

In that article, the authors essentially argue for a production system that finds out what different customers want and then provides it to them. In meeting this challenge, telecommunications could play an instrumental role. One example is a farmer who established a computer connection with an overseas broker to find out about garbanzo bean yields in a country that completed its harvest in February. With this immediate knowledge, he could then decide whether or not to plant garbanzo beans on his own farm in early March. By utilizing containerized cargo shipping methods, he could then build a market identity for his particular crops. And by meeting consumers' demand, he would be in a good position to compete for future orders (Ochs, 1986). This same farmer learned via a computer bulletin board (accessed through his personal computer) that a Middle Eastern country was seeking to buy lentils. In collaboration with other farmers he was able to respond with a direct bid. In Alaska, once a satellite earth station was installed at a fish packing plant in the Aleutian Islands, the business was able to fill orders from its headquarters faster and to change the type of fish caught in response to fluctuations in New York prices. Trappers, once hostage to the village store, can now compare prices at city auction houses before selling their furs (Hudson, 1984).

Of course, instantaneous information is also available to buyers of farm produce. Iowa Beef Processors (IBP) uses a satellite network which allows their buyers in the field to keep in touch with the home office so that they can find out the price they should offer to cattle growers, the quantity they should buy, and the optimal delivery date. Besides trying to obtain the lowest possible price, IBP schedules cattle deliveries to keep its processing plants operating at near capacity (Stevenson, 1981).

The growing information intensity of U.S. agriculture can be seen in the flourishing network of computer networks and databases, including, for example, AGRICOLA, AgriData, and CMN. (See Glossary for further descriptions.) Many states have developed their own computer networks and software for farmers and ranchers. The clientele for these new services includes farmers, extension agents, agribusiness executives, research scientists, college instructors, high school teachers, farm management consultants and USDA personnel (Hudson and Burch, 1988).

Rebuilding a competitive agriculture will require rethinking what is being produced for whom and building new overseas networks to allow farmers to exploit niche markets. To do this, farmers will need information technologies that help them identify market opportunities, make instant contact with commodities futures markets, and obtain "fresher" market data than most farm periodicals can provide. These changes will require a modern, high-quality telecommunications infrastructure.

Services Businesses

As we have noted, services are the dominant source of employment in rural America and the sector that is likely to grow most rapidly. More than any other sector of the rural community, service activities are information intensive. Frequently, information represents both the input to their activities as well as the output. If job growth is to occur in rural America, it seems most likely to occur because of capturing these potentially footloose industries.

Nationwide, the computerization of services is continuing apace. There were 30 million computer work stations in 1987, a number that is expected to double by 1995 so that nine of ten white collar workers will be so equipped. Against this background it is hard to imagine a strong rural service economy without sophisticated computer capabilities. Further, the next revolution in the computerization of America, still in its initial high cost phase, is the networking of computers across families of businesses and sectors of an economy so that information flows quickly from where it originates to where it is needed.

Numerous examples already demonstrate how a business with good telecommunications can succeed from a rural location. An insurance company operates effectively from rural northern Minnesota. A cookie company based in a small Utah town operates more than one hundred outlets in shopping malls throughout the United States. A computer software company with worldwide sales operates from a remote area of Idaho. A major mail order retailer operates from Maine and relies on suppliers from the rural Northeast.

"Telecommuting"—working at home using telecommunications—is gaining wider acceptance. A major catalog sales firm has more than 100 employees working out of their homes to accept long-distance orders. Although most of these workers happen to be in metropolitan areas, it is equally possible to answer calls to 800 numbers, process insurance claims or reorganize financial data from households located hundreds of miles away from the employer.

The development of such innovative service businesses has been hampered in rural America by inadequate telecommunications: a lack of digital switching, an inability to operate modems on party lines, poor quality telephone line connections which slow data transmission, or the prohibitive costs of having to call long distance to the nearest city in order to connect with a toll-free data network. Revamping rural telecommunications could lay a foundation to expand the information sector of the rural economy.

Tourism

At one time rural tourism thrived on its rustic, get-away-from-it-all qualities. Increasingly, visitors to rural locales are attracted by destination resorts, where they expect standard urban amenities such as toll-free reservations, multiple-channel television, pay television services, facsimile machines and direct-dial long-distance service with a choice of carriers.

Telecommunications are also important for resort management and marketing. An 800 number, telex machine and computer terminal are vital for reservations. Like any business, resorts also use telecommunications for logistics, ordering supplies and general management. In many cases, telecommunications can improve operating efficiencies of rural tourism enterprises—even backpacking in wilderness areas—through time-sensitive pricing and marketing to boost tourism during off-season and low-occupancy periods.

Small Businesses

Small business plays a major role in rural economies, whether in manufacturing, services or agriculture. Their entrepreneurial spirit and flexible attitudes are important to successful rural development, and their small size makes them appropriate for small communities. Yet in an economy in which

75 percent of business products and services are exposed to international competition, small businesses face special difficulties in competing.

Fortunately, telecommunications offer a rare form of empowerment for small businesses. For example, small businesses can use modem-equipped computers to access electronic bulletin boards to obtain information that large companies normally secure through their market analysis departments or through their presence in multiple locations. Telecommunications can help small businesses obtain requests for bids in a timely manner, specialized market analyses for crafting business strategies, and other timely information essential to competing in the global marketplace.

Large companies operating in rural areas can usually solve their communications problems by purchasing satellite connections or special telephone line installations. Small companies usually cannot afford this option, or the option is simply not available because of insufficient local demand. Small businesses in urban areas can often obtain access to sophisticated telecommunications facilities such as optical fiber by riding on the coattails of larger businesses. But demand for such telecommunications is too low in rural areas to justify the investment by local telephone companies.

The result is a cruel irony: new telecommunications now offer rich new development possibilities for rural America and new ways of overcoming the "rural penalty." Yet the dynamics of private investment in telecommunications make it unlikely that rural communities will in fact share in the bounties of the Information Age. A modest commitment by government, however, can help solve this conundrum.

Services for Rural Residents

A developed telecommunications infrastructure can also contribute to more efficient, effective and high-quality services. For example, the rural population as a whole benefits if shuttle bus operators can communicate with their headquarters via radio or cellular telephone; if health paraprofessionals can contact physicians in cities or regional centers; if agricultural extension agents can query outside experts to answer farmers' questions; and if students can interact with distant instructors to study subjects not offered by local teachers. Besides enhancing quality of life, these information exchanges can yield many economic benefits such as new efficiencies in services, fewer patient evacuations, higher crop yields and reduced student dropout and failure rates.

Transportation

Large inter-city buses represent the last bastion of public passenger transportation for many rural towns. Unfortunately, in this era of differentiated markets and targeted products and services, it is something of an anachronism to have buses running standard routes, making frequent stops whether or not there are passengers, and arriving at a single downtown city terminal. As with many mass society-oriented services, the more one tries to meet the average needs of the average consumer, the more likely one will not meet the needs of anyone in particular.

A more realistic model for serving contemporary travel needs may be the flexible, point-to-point services that airport vans and overnight delivery services are now developing in rural communities. The essence of these services is home pickup and delivery to the desired destination; two-way radio communication allows last-minute changes in routes. (Cellular telephone contacts to customers' homes and businesses could make these services even more useful.)

Telecommunications not only helps make transportation services more responsive to customers, but also enables carriers to budget their time and minimize mileage costs, thereby maximizing revenues. Telecommunications could also allow rural transportation systems to deploy their vehicles more efficiently by soliciting advance travel reservations. Overhead costs could be cut by using ticket agents who handle all customers by telephone.

Health Care

Telecommunications already plays an important role in emergencies and health services worldwide, but it is especially valuable to rural areas where distances are so great. Studies of rural telephone calls in several countries show that about five percent of all calls were for emergencies and medical reasons (Hudson, 1984). While this figure is higher than might be expected in the U.S., the indirect benefits of emergency communications, in saving lives and reducing suffering, can be significant.

Health care in the rural U.S. is currently in a state of crisis, as a result of several trends. One trend is the increased reliance on specialists for the diagnosis and treatment of medical problems. Another is the increased costs to rural hospitals of purchasing and maintaining equipment needed for modern medical care. The problems faced by these hospitals are low occupancy rates and too few specialized doctors to warrant the cost of equipment. At the same time, new insurance rules are limiting hospital stays, forcing those rural patients who need specialized care to leave urban hospitals promptly and return to their distant homes, even though they may need close monitoring.

A modern telecommunications infrastructure offers potential solutions to these problems. The availability of expert systems, available via computer modems, can enable general practitioners to diagnose and treat their patients with the help of specialists, without sending their patients to urban hospitals. Similarly, if post-surgery patients can be hooked up to monitoring systems connected to urban medical centers, they may be able to return to their distant homes sooner and with less risk than before—while saving on the cost of a hospital stay.

Over the past decade, experiments and pilot projects in "telemedicine" have demonstrated the feasibility of remote examination and monitoring of patients, and of transmissions of X-rays and electrocardiograms (Bashur, 1983). In many rural areas throughout the country, health care providers actively use telecommunications technologies for consultations and continuing education.

Another cost-saving yet effective means of delivering primary health care is the use of paraprofessionals in rural locations. Telecommunications links between rural clinics and regional hospitals or health centers can be used for consultation and supervision. In Alaska, village health aides are in daily contact with doctors in regional hospitals via an audio conferencing satellite circuit, using village earth stations also used for telephony and broadcasting. The system allows doctors to oversee the aides' diagnoses and treatment plans; many patients who previously would have had to be evacuated to a hospital can now safely remain in the village. A computerized recordkeeping system allows medical staff to access and update patient records from any location. It also allows staff to monitor people who need special attention, such as patients with pacemakers or tuberculosis, or children requiring vaccinations.

The economic benefits to a village can be enormous. Compared with the costs of travel to a distant city and hospitalization, telemedicine can be 21 times cheaper for patients in rural communities and more than 40 times cheaper for patients in the most isolated areas (Hudson, 1982).

Education

A recent Office of Technology Assessment report (1988) on the American economy in transition notes that about 50 percent of the new jobs created between 1980 and 1986 went to people with at least three years of college education. The report argues that an educated population is as essential as were infrastructure investments of the past, such as canals, railroads, and electrification.

Perhaps the biggest challenge facing rural education is how to provide specialized instruction. Small high schools are unable to offer a wide array of vocational and college preparatory classes; higher education opportunities are often nonexistent. The problem has grown worse as the rural population has declined in the 1980s and the baby boom generation has matured, causing enrollments in rural schools to drop. As urban schools move ahead with innovative programs such as lifelong learning and computer instruction, rural education may lag further behind national norms.

Telecommunications technology offers many solutions beyond reconsolidation of school districts, the path often chosen in earlier years of this century. Rather than transporting students for even greater distances to create a critical mass of students, telecommunications can take educational opportunities to students, and reach adults as well, with interactive and broadcasting services.

One successful distance-learning model is the TI-IN network, based in Texas, which uses satellite communications to reach rural schools. TI-IN offers specialized courses in foreign languages, mathematics and science, enrichment courses, and staff development programs. At the graduate level, the National Technological University (NTU) offers satellite-transmitted technical courses to employees at their workplaces throughout the country; they do not have to leave the worksite to go to graduate school.

Adult education and career development are common goals of distance learners. The Wisconsin Educational Telecommunications Network (WETN), an audio-conferencing network, has offered hundreds of courses to adults throughout the state. Athabasca University of Alberta, Canada, uses audio teleconferencing to augment correspondence courses taken by adults living in small towns, farms, and isolated northern settlements. The Teleconferencing Network of Texas (TNT) offers audio teleseminars for nurses at more than 70 rural Texan hospitals. The system allows the nurses to supplement their correspondence studies, take courses that otherwise would not be available to them, and encourages them to remain at rural hospitals.

Rural residents without post-secondary educational institutions may benefit most from satellite-distributed instruction. One example is the Learning Channel, an outgrowth of the Appalachian Community Services Network (ACSN) experiment launched by the Appalachian Regional Commission a decade ago. At first the Learning Channel provided continuing and career education to small centers in Appalachia. It now disseminates adult education courses to households throughout the country via satellite distribution to local cable systems.

6. Rural Telecommunications and Quality of Life

Many rural areas are discovering just how important quality-of-life attributes can be in spurring economic development.

Increasingly, "footloose" industries, tourists, retirees and owners of second homes are moving to high-amenity rural areas because of the pleasant natural environments, recreational facilities, friendly neighborhoods, and less frantic pace.

But the very isolation which enhances quality of life can also impede economic development. Footloose industries need to communicate with urban businesses; resorts need to offer reservation and cable TV services; retirees from urban areas are often accustomed to such services as electronic banking and cable television. Enhanced telecommunications can preserve quality of life while attracting new enterprises that develop the local economy.

Retirement

More older people are moving to rural areas for their retirement, bringing with them special needs and the wealth to satisfy them. Telecommunications can help meet many of these needs. For example, rural retirees naturally want to maintain close contact with friends and relatives in distant cities. As the society ages, more older people will combine retirement with occasional work or investment activities, both of which may require frequent telephone or facsimile communications with business associates in distant cities. Indeed, the extensive use of fax machines by businesses may soon spread to the public at large. Already some mail order businesses accept facsimile orders from customers. Given their wealth and inclinations, rural retirees will come to expect more sophisticated telecommunications.

Civic Participation

Telecommunications can help enable rural residents to participate more directly in government deliberations. One successful example is Alaska's Legislative Teleconferencing Network (LTN). The system allows towns with legislative information offices to conduct audio conferences, talk to their elected representatives, or access a computer network to track down the status of legislation and then retrieve the bill via facsimile transmission. Perhaps the most successful LTN service has been teleconferencing of legislative hearings. Through LTN, residents who cannot afford to travel to Juneau, the state capital, can testify at hearings from their home communities. When the full legislature is not in session, legislators can use the LTN to participate in committee meetings from their home districts (Walp, 1982).

Information and Cultural Enrichment

Libraries are important information and cultural resources in rural communities. Yet they cannot provide a service now increasingly common at many urban libraries, namely online access via telephone lines to databases around the country. One impediment to offering this service is the lack of high-quality telephone lines for data transmission.

Even where these lines exist in rural regions, however, the cost of using them may be prohibitive if a phone call crosses local service area boundaries or jurisdictions of more than one telephone company. A rural library in Washington state, for example, found that it would have to pay $8,000 per year for online access to an "information gateway" (a telecommunications service in a nearby urban center that provides access to direct links with various database services).

Access to television channels, via both broadcast and cable, is another important cultural need for rural regions. Despite complaints about TV as a cultural wasteland, television remains an integral part of our lives and a window on the world. Besides providing entertainment and popular culture, it is a rich source of news, information, and education for all ages.

Although cable television is rapidly penetrating most incorporated areas, even in rural counties, little has been done to assure its availability in unincorporated rural areas. It is important that the city limits no longer be a demarcation between those who can and cannot enjoy access to cable television. Although satellite antennas offer one possible solution, they are unaffordable for many households. One solution is to allow a broader waiver for unincorporated rural areas from FCC rules prohibiting cross-ownership of telephone and cable television services. (See Chapter Four, Section 7.)

Quality of Rural Life

Telecommunications alone will obviously not stem rural migration to cities. Yet telecommunications can enhance the quality of rural living and, to that extent, contribute to the personal and social well-being of rural residents. In the early days, some thought that the telephone would stem the flight from the farm to the city. Obviously, as noted in the previous chapter, urban migration did not cease. But as Ithiel de Sola Pool pointed out, the telephone, along with the automobile, electricity, and mass media, may have stemmed the pace of a movement that was largely determined by agricultural economics, namely, the increase in agricultural productivity and the growth of urban employment (Pool, 1984). Now telecommunications, by contributing to a more diversified rural economy, can give rural residents greater security and freedom of choice in their lives.

7. Summary

Numerous studies confirm that telecommunications can improve productivity and efficiency in business; enhance the quality of social services; and extend social, cultural and economic opportunities more equitably throughout rural regions. The challenge ahead is to forge a more deliberate, comprehensive policy to build an adequate telecommunications infrastructure for rural America.

══════ FOUR

TELECOMMUNICATIONS
POLICY ISSUES AFFECTING
RURAL AMERICA

The 1980s have been a time of dramatic transition in U.S. telecommunications policy. The engine of change has been new technologies—digital switching, fiber optics, satellite transmission, and others. Change has also been propelled by the much-noted convergence of computer and telecommunications technologies, which rendered prior regulatory policies either impractical or unfair.

As mentioned in Chapter One, regulators chose not to stifle emerging competition in telecommunications. The result has been the breakup of AT&T, the gradual deregulation and restructuring of telecommunications markets, and the creation of a new regulatory regime to oversee the transition to a more open, competitive marketplace.

The new FCC policies have been designed to bring new products, services and efficiencies to business and residential consumers. The policies are also meant to speed the transition to a marketplace driven by entrepreneurialism, innovation, quality service and products, and prices that better reflect actual costs. Already the deregulatory environment has helped spawn competing long-distance telephone services and lower long-distance rates; new varieties of phone equipment; and new voice, video and data transmission services such as teleconferencing and facsimile document transmission.

However people may feel about the new deregulatory environment, there is no going back to the regulated monopoly system. Yet it is important to recognize the serious hardships that the transition to a competitive telecommunications marketplace is creating for rural areas. Small rural telephone carriers surviving on the fringes of the national telephone network compare their plight to that of the last person in the children's game of "crack the whip"; policies that ripple past those in the middle of the market have exaggerated whiplash effects on those at the end.

Rural areas benefitted from the prior regulated monopoly through internal cross-subsidies that transferred some of the costs of rural service to urban subscribers. Now, telecommunications competition is creating pressure for every route and service to pay its own way. Without carefully planned transition policies, the longstanding policy goal of providing everyone with affordable POTS, "plain old telephone service," could be threatened, especially in rural areas.

The most severe potential danger from deregulation may not be recognized until some point in the future when rural America discovers that, apart from a few residual industries, it is unprepared to compete in the national economy. Unable to afford an improved telecommunications infrastructure—which would include digital switching, high-quality transmission lines, software-enhanced services, and other improvements—major portions of rural America may well be consigned to steady economic decline. With that infrastructure, ailing rural economies would at least have the opportunity to better themselves.

What follows are brief discussions of key telecommunications policy issues affecting rural America.

1. Access Charges

One result of the breakup of AT&T and new competition in long-distance service is the subscriber "access charge" (otherwise known as the subscriber line charge) that all telephone subscribers, urban and rural, must now pay. This surcharge, currently $3.50 per month per residential telephone line in most locations, is a fee by which users pay for access to local telephone exchanges and hence to long-distance services. The fee pays part of the "non-traffic sensitive" (fixed) costs of equipment required for both local and long-distance calls.

Before the divestiture of the Bell operating companies from AT&T, the more-or-less arbitrary allocation of costs between local and long distance mattered less. After all, most of the money went into different pockets of the same company anyway. Nevertheless, allocations of costs had to be made between FCC-regulated interstate services and state-regulated local services. In each jurisdiction, the rates subscribers paid had to be approved by the regulators, who disallowed rates that exceeded costs by more than the allowed rate of return.

In the years prior to divestiture, actual costs of long-distance service had been declining because of major technical advances, and local costs had been edging up. As a way of avoiding unpopular local rate increases, regulators and carriers over time agreed to allocate more of the local fixed costs to interstate long distance. That way, long-distance rates did not decrease as much as they would have otherwise, and both rural and urban residents got the benefit of cheaper local rates.

Under new FCC policies being phased in over eight years from 1986, the allocation of costs between local and long distance telephone user is changing substantially. By 1994, a maximum of 25 percent of the non-traffic-sensitive costs will be allocated to long-distance interstate calls. To help reduce the interstate allocation to 25 percent, subscriber access charges of $3.50 per month are being added directly to local phone bills. To help high-cost rural carriers deal with their additional cost burdens as the prior subsidy is phased out, the FCC has established a "universal service fund" to be paid out of long-distance revenues.

Long-distance carriers pay a different set of carrier access charges to local phone companies to pay for the remaining costs allocated to long distance but not covered by subscribers' access charges. The carriers' access charges (which are folded into their long-distance rates to consumers) are pooled and distributed by the National Exchange Carrier Association (NECA). (For information on NECA, see Appendix 1.)

Rural residents benefit from the new rate system through lower long-distance rates. But their overall benefit may be reduced or eliminated by higher local phone rates, the result of the new reallocation of costs and rising local costs. Heavy interstate long-distance users obviously enjoy a greater benefit from the new system than users who rarely or never use long distance. In short, there are winners and losers under the new rate system; the complicated transition affects everyone.

2. Long-Distance Competition

While the new access charge policies are meant to encourage competition, lower costs and improve service, these benefits have been slow to come to rural areas. This is because competitive long-distance carriers have chosen to expand their networks into the more lucrative urban areas first. But even if long-distance carriers decide to serve rural regions, the local telephone exchange carrier must first upgrade its switching hardware, acquire the necessary software, and install a special switch and lines providing competing carriers "equal access" to phone users. Equal access permits each subscriber to select which long distance company to use without having to dial a lot of extra numbers or place a long-distance call to reach a carrier other than AT&T. Providing the capability for subscribers to use different long-distance carriers can be prohibitively expensive for small local exchanges.

To help solve this problem in an economical way, small telephone companies can aggregate their long-distance traffic at a central, shared equal access switch. (Of course, they must provide the initial capital cost of the shared switch and the lines connecting their subscribers to that switch.) This approach is being taken in Iowa, where an organization called Iowa Network Services plans to provide equal access to competitive long-distance carriers through a centralized, shared switch beginning in 1989. Other innovative arrangements may have to be devised if other rural subscribers are to reap the full benefits of a policy for which they are already paying the costs.

Apart from the costly capital investment needed to gain access to long-distance carriers, many rural regions are disadvantaged by the historical jurisdictional boundaries that determine which calls will be considered local and which long distance. In the current telecommunications regulatory structure, the United States is divided into 164 areas, called Local Access Transport Areas, or LATAs. The FCC has authorized inter-LATA long-distance competition if the LATAs are in different states. Intrastate inter-LATA competition has been authorized by most (but not all) of the states with more than one LATA. But intra-LATA long-distance service is, in most states, still a monopoly of the local exchange carriers. Hence the irony that a shorter-distance call within a large LATA may cost more than a transcontinental call using a competitive long-distance carrier. Rural subscribers in large LATAs are particularly penalized by this anomaly.

3. Long-Distance Rates

City dwellers can usually obtain the information and services they need through local telephone calls. Rural residents must often make long-distance calls, which naturally makes long-distance rates a matter of great concern. This concern is growing because rural users fear a major policy change in how long-distance rates will be set. Currently, long-distance rates are based on nationwide average costs. Yet since costs per line are much higher on rural routes (because they serve fewer people than on interurban routes, which serve many more people), rural subscribers are the primary beneficiaries of this policy.

Although the FCC has reaffirmed its support for nationwide rate averaging, rural telephone carriers are concerned that the general trend toward cost-based pricing will eventually lead to "de-averaged" rates—and higher prices for rural areas. Already the pressure to de-average rates is intensifying because of the decision by Bell operating companies (BOCs) to stop pooling their costs after April 1, 1989. The FCC permitted the BOCs to withdraw from the nationwide average cost pools on the condition they contribute funds to the pool sufficient to not disadvantage the small rural carriers. The net effect is that the BOCs no longer subsidize each other, but still have to support the smaller carriers. Rural carriers worry that there may be further pressures to reduce that subsidy, thereby forcing higher rates on their subscribers.

Rural carriers are also concerned that Federal Judge Harold Greene, who oversees the AT&T consent decree that broke up the Bell system, will permit the BOCs to compete for long-distance services using de-averaged rates, thereby driving up prices for their rural subscribers. They also worry that Judge Greene may relax the equipment manufacturing restrictions on BOCs, which could potentially reduce or eliminate competitive sources of supply for rural carriers.

Even if it were agreed that the long run policy goal should be cost-based or competitively determined pricing on each long distance route, fairness would demand transition policies to cushion the inevitable blows to rural areas. Regulatory policies that foster a competitive environment for telecommunications usually hurt rural areas most, because the lower call volume in rural regions makes it less attractive to long-distance carriers.

If rates are allowed to be de-averaged at some future date, fairness demands a set of transition policies that help rural carriers install the switching equipment needed to gain access to the range of long-distance carriers. Otherwise, rural areas would have none of the benefits of competition and instead would get substantially higher prices without any choice of long-distance carrier.

Transition policies are also needed to encourage rural carriers to install lower cost technology (including communication satellite and radio telephone technology where appropriate) on their most expensive routes. One impediment to installation of lower cost technology fell in February 1989 when the FCC ruled that radio telephone technology should be classified as network equipment. This means that a rural telephone exchange can now put the costs of this technology into its rate base, making it more affordable for rural carriers and less costly for individual subscribers.

It will take time for rural carriers to recover through depreciation charges the costs of expensive wireline technology installed under prior regulatory assumptions and at a time when there were few, if any, technical alternatives. It will also take time to introduce new policies that will make it economically feasible for rural carriers to install lower-cost technologies, such as radio telephones, on rural routes.

4. Depreciation Charges

One of the major components of telephone rates, both rural and urban, is the depreciation charged to recover the costs of the capital equipment installed in the network. Depreciation policies are important because they affect the rate at which rural areas can afford to install new and improved telecommunications facilities.

One way state regulators kept local telephone rates down was to give the equipment a longer working life, for depreciation accounting purposes. Thus, if equipment were depreciated over 40 years (to use a simplified example), the depreciation charges included in the rates for any single year would be four times less than if the same equipment were depreciated over 10 years.

Unfortunately, these accounting rules also make it harder to replace equipment with new and better equipment. It doesn't make sense to take obsolete equipment out of service if doing so means that the original cost of the equipment will not be recovered. Longer depreciation schedules were an acceptable strategy to keep rates low when the rate of telecommunications innovation was modest. Now the depreciation policies are making it all the more difficult to replace older equipment.

To help solve this problem, the FCC ordered accelerated depreciation schedules and attempted to preempt state policy on the issue. But the FCC was overruled by the U.S. Supreme Court, which held that only the states could control depreciation schedules on that portion of telephone equipment allocated to state jurisdiction. As a result, state depreciation policies may be a critical factor in whether rural telephone carriers will be able to provide newer model digital switches, the linch pin of enhanced telecommunications services.

5. Universal Service

Universal service—that is, voice telephone service accessible to all U.S. households that wish to purchase it—has been the cornerstone of U.S. telecommunications policy for more than 50 years. The internal cross-subsidies and nationwide rate averaging were policies deliberately adopted to achieve that goal.

The FCC estimates that by March 1988, 92.9 percent of the 91 million U.S. households had at least one telephone. Some 94.6 percent of households had access to a telephone either at home or elsewhere. Approximately 6.5 million households (7.1 per cent of the total households) are still without basic telephone service either because they are located in rural regions where it simply is not available or because they cannot afford it. The FCC estimates that 27 percent of households with an annual income of under $5,000 are without service. Our analysis estimates that 183,000 U.S. households are without telephone service because their rural location is too remote to permit service currently. (See Chapter Five.)

For the most remote locations, communications satellite and terrestrial radio telephone may be the only affordable means of providing telephone service; subsidizing conventional wireline technology is often far too costly. A new FCC-authorized radio telephone service, Basic Exchange Telephone Radio Service (BETRS), now provides an excellent alternative to wire-line technology for many rural locations.

Rural carriers and their subscribers could be substantially hurt by the FCC-ordered transition to the 25 percent cap on local fixed-cost allocations to the interstate jurisdiction. If the resulting higher local cost allocations were all passed on to subscribers, many who now have service could no longer afford it. Therefore, to further the goal of universal service, the FCC ordered the establishment of a special universal service fund paid from long distance revenues and administered by NECA (see Appendix 1). These funds are allocated to the particularly high-cost service areas to help keep phone rates affordable for subscribers in those areas.

The FCC has also authorized a lifeline service fund, subject to matching by state regulators, to help low- income subscribers maintain basic telephone service. It was recently determined that many low-income households go without telephone service not because of the monthly rates, but because of high installation charges and deposits. In response, the FCC also established the "Link Up America" program in 1987 to provide federal assistance for one-half the cost of residential installation, up to $30. The subsidy is available to participating telephone carriers in states that have approved participation in the program.

Although the original goal of universal voice telephone service has been largely met, the new competitive environment threatens to reverse previous gains unless new policies are adopted. Since its inception in the Communications Act of 1934, universal service has never implied an entitlement program under which U.S. residents would have a right to telephone service at government expense. Rather, the goal, now as then, is to ensure that the structure of the industry makes telephone service universally accessible and affordable.

6. Price Caps

One key proposal on the 1989 telecommunications policy agenda is to substitute price caps for rate of return regulation. For more than 50 years, federal and state regulators have had to review and approve proposed rate requests based on a "cost-plus" formula. The rates cannot exceed the amount needed to recover costs plus a return on the capital investment sufficient to pay the interest expense on borrowed funds and to provide equity investors with a return on their investment.

Regulatory and free market economists have argued that this scheme of regulation is not efficient because it does not provide the carriers with incentives to lower costs. The carriers are permitted to determine the largest components of the prices (capital and operating costs) and regulators merely determine what constitutes a fair rate of return after costs are recovered. Critics charge that this cost-plus regulatory system leads to over-investment ("gold-plating") because the larger the base of investment costs on which the carriers can receive a percentage of profit, the larger their profits will be. Under such a system, carriers may have little or no incentive to lower costs through more efficient equipment or operating procedures.

The alternative—price caps—would modify rate of return regulation to permit price increases only up to a maximum that is less than the rate of inflation. In other words, in order for telephone carriers to maintain current levels of return on investment, they would have to achieve cost reductions and productivity gains. If they achieved productivity gains greater than the target sum (the difference between the inflation rate and the allowed price increase), then the rate of return to the carriers' investors could increase. In theory, such a regulatory policy would provide more incentive for carriers to operate efficiently than under the current cost-plus policy. For this very reason, many carriers would like to see the implementation of price cap regulation.

Price cap regulation could also have a substantial impact on the quality of service. Under rate of return regulation, carriers needed approval from regulators for major investments being added to the rate base. These approvals were intended to protect consumers from price increases resulting from unnecessary investment. Under price cap regulation, the carrier incentives are different. Instead of regulating additions to the rate base, regulators will need to regulate service quality to protect subscribers from cost cutting that impairs service.

In 1989, AT&T became the first U.S. carrier subject to price cap regulation instead of rate of return regulation. There is a longer history of price cap regulation in the United Kingdom, where price caps have been used to regulate the rates of British Telecom (BT), which was privatized after decades as part of the British Post Office. A recent report by Oftel, the regulator of British Telecom, has confirmed that service quality fell under price cap regulation, although some analysts blame an engineering staff strike (Rudd, 1988).

Price cap regulation is yet another change to which rural carriers must adjust. To the extent that rural carriers are receiving cross-subsidies (from other carriers with which they connect to complete long-distance calls for their rural subscribers), pressures may grow to reduce those subsidies. Since the current mechanism for cross-subsidy involves various allocations of costs and cost averaging, it will be essential to maintain records of the underlying cost information from price cap carriers as well as rate of return regulated carriers. Otherwise, an entirely new mechanism of subsidy for rural carriers would have to be devised and implemented.

As with other recent regulatory changes, price cap telecommunications regulation may be deemed to be in the public interest. Nevertheless, special mechanisms must be in place at the time of the change to protect rural carriers and their subscribers from suddenly inflated cost allocations and the potentially reduced quality of service from the carriers with which they connect to complete long-distance calls. For rural subscribers in areas served by carriers that elect price cap regulation, special quality of service regulations may also be required.

7. Telephone/Cable Television Cross-Ownership

In many communities, two sets of communication cables connect local homes and businesses, one offering point-to-point telephone voice service and another offering video (broadcast and cable TV) and audio services. Even though the two systems do not currently compete, both of them are capable of handling data communication. As the telephone and cable industries move to optical fiber, the technical capabilities of the two transmission systems could converge further.

Advocates of competition applaud such developments as good for the economy and consumers. Others complain that it is inefficient to have two costly, duplicative sets of communication cables, both of which require access to public rights of way, separate line connections to subscribers, and separate inside wiring. Still others point out that the most economical solution for locations that do not already have both telephone and cable TV service (primarily rural areas) is a common set of cables.

Congress made its choice in this debate when it enacted the Cable Communications Policy Act of 1984, placing limits on the types of cooperation and competition allowed between cable television and telephone carriers. The FCC has imposed further restrictions through a ban on cross-ownership of cable television and telephone businesses. Recognizing that these rules simply do not make sense for the sparse populations of rural areas, Congress and the FCC provided a waiver for rural areas (defined by the FCC as communities with no more than 2,500 people).

What makes this issue still timely is a pending FCC rulemaking which would expand the waiver. Some petitioners have suggested that the rural exception be broadened to include: 1) all nonurban areas not served by both telephone and cable TV services; 2) all areas served by telephone carriers that borrow funds from the Rural Electrification Administration (REA); 3) all service areas with fewer than 60 telephone subscribers per route mile; and 4) all communities of no more than 10,000 people. It has also been suggested that the FCC should broaden the allowable affiliation between cable and telephone companies to the maximum extent permitted by the Cable Act.

Whatever the merits of keeping the telephone and cable TV industries separate in urban areas, the industries should be permitted to join together in rural areas. Without such joint economies of scale, affordable video, voice and data service may not be available at all to many rural residents.

8. Open Network Architecture

Another telecommunications issue on the FCC agenda concerns how to forge a new competitive information services market that would rely on the monopoly transmission channels of local telephone carriers.

Information providers worry that if telephone carriers are allowed to provide information services, carriers will use their local transmission monopoly to compete unfairly. They argue that without effective, regulated access to the monopoly communication channels and without well-defined technical interfaces and rules for competition, they would be seriously handicapped in competing with telephone carriers to provide value-added information services (such as access to databases and electronic mail systems).

Some telephone carriers retort that it would be unfair for them to provide the "electronic highways" for information services of unproven commercial viability unless they can share a piece of the pie, by providing their own information services in addition to the underlying transmission facilities. For example, they argue that they should be permitted to provide their telephone directories, both white and yellow pages, in electronic form. Furthermore, carriers argue that they may not be able to provide a suitable electronic highway and gateways if they cannot develop the sophisticated understanding of the business that comes from being a part of it.

At this juncture, there is a chicken or egg problem that prevents the information services and transport services from emerging as a new industry; neither can be economical without the other. To help break the impasse and "jump-start" the market, telephone carriers argue that they should be permitted to develop and offer some information services via their local transmission systems. But such a move would require changing FCC rules and the AT&T consent decree, both of which prohibit Bell operating companies from offering electronic information services.

A further unresolved problem results from the near impossibility of distinguishing between digital information processing and digital information transmission and switching, given that the technology of digital information switches is virtually identical to that used by computers in data processing. In a series of "computer inquiries," the FCC found that it would be impossible to enforce a defensible definitional boundary between information processing and information transmission.

The latest FCC attempt to resolve this issue is to establish a common set of technical interface standards, called Open Network Architecture (ONA). The scheme would allow information providers and information processing businesses to have fair and equal access to the parts of the network they need without cumbersome or proprietary interfaces and without being forced to pay for "bundled services" that include more than they need.

Resolving this issue is important for the U.S. economy because electronically accessible information services may play a key role in achieving productivity gains and enhancing our international competitiveness. But such benefits cannot be achieved until a regulatory framework is established that will permit the simultaneous emergence of information services and the electronic highways to carry them. Just as the emergence of facsimile machines as a major tool of business communication was delayed until after appropriate technology and universal standards were accepted, so new digital information services will depend on appropriate technology and universal standards.

A national open standard for access to digital information would have substantial benefits for both rural and urban telephone subscribers and their respective economies. But there is a distinct risk that only urban areas will get ONA service, as the FCC warned in its comment on proposed schedules for the introduction of ONA services by the Bell operating companies: "We caution the BOCs not to assume, without compelling evidence to the contrary, that large cities are the only places where market demand will support ONA services." (FCC ONA order, 1988, p. 189.)

FIVE

A PORTRAIT OF THE TELECOMMUNICATIONS INFRASTRUCTURE IN RURAL AMERICA TODAY

No work to improve rural telecommunications can be undertaken without first understanding its current state of (under) development. What does the rural telecommunications stock consist of, and how rapidly is it being upgraded? What types of services are currently available to rural businesses and residents? What are the likely future trends?

To help sketch such a portrait, Economic Management Consultants International, Inc. (EMCI) conducted several detailed economic and statistical analyses. (All numerical estimates in this chapter not otherwise attributed were the result of EMCI calculations.) This chapter provides fresh insights to five key issues:

- What is the extent of telephone penetration in rural households? Why do households without telephones not have telephone service?
- How common are multiparty telephone lines, and what is the rate of upgrade from multi- to single-party service?
- How available are enhanced telecommunications services, which typically require digital telephone switches? What is the rate of upgrade to digital from analog systems?
- What is the quality of transmission lines?
- What is the likely future penetration of mobile cellular telephone service in rural areas?

1. Universal Access

While the U.S. has made great strides in its goal of providing universal access to telephone service, there are still a significant number of households without telephone service. Recent surveys conducted by the Census and analyzed by the FCC estimate that in 1986 there were approximately 6.8 million households without telephone service. It is widely believed that these households are located in remote areas of the country where the provision of telephone service through traditional copper wire is not possible or is prohibitively expensive. Yet, in fact, most households without telephone service are located in areas in which telephone service is available.

An estimated 64 percent of all households are located in metropolitan areas, where access to telephone service is highly likely. A closer analysis reveals that income is a far better predictor of whether a household will have telephone service than urban/rural location. The FCC has estimated that only 7.8 percent of all households did not have telephone service in 1986. Among households with an annual income less than $5,000, however, 27 percent did not have telephone service. By contrast, less than one percent of households with incomes greater than $75,000 did not have telephone service. Table 4 below shows how telephone service varies with income levels.

The FCC has also found a high correlation between receipt of food stamps and households without telephone service. Thirty-one percent of households receiving food stamps did not have telephone service, while under six percent of households not receiving food stamps did not have telephone service.

Using the correlation between income and households without telephone service, we developed economic models that estimate the number of households without telephone service within a given area, based on local income levels. We found that the percentage of households without telephone service is most closely correlated with the percentage of households living in poverty (as defined by Census Bureau statistics for both income and family size). By isolating the number of households that do not have telephone service due to poverty, it is possible to assess

Table 4   Households without Telephone Service, by Level of Income (000s)

Household Income	Number of Households	Households w/service	Households w/o service	Percent w/o service
Under 5,000	6,851	5,026	1,825	26.6
$ 5,000 - 7,500	6,028	4,970	1,058	17.6
$ 7,500 - 10,000	4,970	4,260	710	14.3
$10,000 - 12,500	5,313	4,690	623	11.7
$12,500 - 15,000	4,800	4,324	476	9.9
$15,000 - 17,500	4,954	4,538	416	8.4
$17,500 - 20,000	4,642	4,341	301	6.5
$20,000 - 22,500	4,801	4,504	297	6.2
$22,500 - 25,000	4,000	3,771	229	5.7
$25,000 - 27,500	3,625	3,486	139	3.8
$27,500 - 30,000	3,919	3,814	105	2.7
$32,500 - 35,000	3,008	2,937	71	2.4
$35,000 - 37,500	3,241	3,165	76	2.3
$37,500 - 40,000	2,474	2,434	40	1.6
$40,000 - 45,000	4,628	4,549	79	1.7
$45,000 - 50,000	3,560	3,507	53	1.5
$50,000 - 60,000	5,184	5,124	60	1.2
$60,000 - 75,000	3,902	3,872	30	0.8
$75,000 and over	3,892	3,863	29	0.7
TOTAL	88,193	81,349	6,844	7.8

Source: Calculations by EMCI; underlying data from U.S. Bureau of the Census and tabulations contained in "Telephone Penetration and Household Characteristics," published by Industry Analysis Division, Common Carrier Bureau, FCC, 1987. Based on 1986 survey data.

how geography alone affects telephone penetration. The distribution of households without telephone service is shown in Figure 6.

We estimate that there are 183,000 households in the U.S. that do not have access to telephone service due to remoteness. Sixty-four percent of all households without telephone service are in metropolitan areas, and the primary reason for lack of service is low income. Thirty-six percent of households without telephone service are in rural areas. Again, the primary reason for lack of service is poverty. Only three percent of all households without telephone service are estimated not to have service due to geographic isolation. (Details of the methodologies used in the analyses are provided in Appendix 2.)

Figure 6   Summary of U.S. Households Without Telephone Service

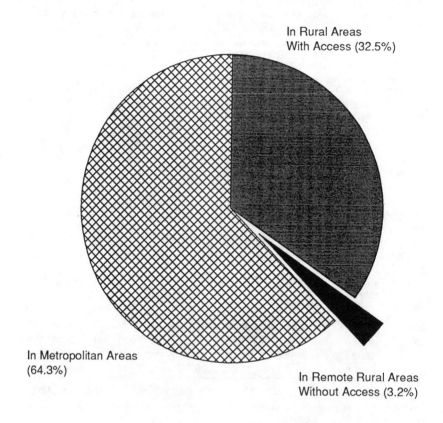

In Rural Areas
With Access (32.5%)

In Metropolitan Areas
(64.3%)

In Remote Rural Areas
Without Access (3.2%)

Source: EMCI, Inc.

For those households that are remote, many could be helped through new radio technologies. Basic Exchange Telecommunications Radio Service (BETRS) is a new service available to local exchange carriers. This technology provides a local subscriber access line via radio instead of traditional copper wire. The initial capital cost for rural telephone carriers to provide radio telephone service is generally closer to $3,000 per subscriber than the $10,000 per subscriber estimates frequently mentioned in rural wireline upgrade analyses.

Figure 6 indicates that the vast majority of households without telephone service lack service because of low incomes rather than because they are remotely located. To reduce significantly the number of households without telephone service, policymakers will have to increase the availability of service to low income households through financial assistance such as lifeline programs.

2. Single-party Telephone Service

There is no single comprehensive source of information that provides an exact breakdown of multiparty line usage in the United States. Two sources can be relied upon in order to obtain accurate estimates: the United States Telephone Association (USTA) and the Rural Electrification Administration (REA). The USTA provides statistics on multiparty lines for both Bell operating companies and independent telephone companies, while REA statistics are derived from its borrowers, mostly independent telephone carriers.

Independent Telephone Companies, Nationwide
As indicated in Table 5, there has been a general decline in the number of multiparty lines among both the Bell operating companies (BOCs) and the independents. The number of access lines has increased from 114 million in 1984 to 127 million in 1987. Over this same period the number of multiparty lines has declined from 4.2 million to 3.1 million. Multiparty

Table 5   Summary of Multiparty Lines (000s)

	Bell System			Independents			Total U.S.		
	Total Lines	Multi-party	Multiparty % Total	Total Lines	Multi-party	Multiparty % Total	Total Lines	Multi-party	Multiparty % Total
1979	81,400	n/a	–	20,078	3,154	15.7	101,478	n/a	–
1980	83,884	n/a	–	20,808	2,954	14.2	104,692	n/a	–
1981	85,987	n/a	–	21,429	2,818	13.2	107,416	n/a	–
1982	86,921	n/a	–	21,672	2,623	12.1	108,593	n/a	–
1983	89,042	n/a	–	22,331	2,282	10.2	111,373	n/a	–
1984	91,454	2,195	2.4	23,020	2,001	8.7	114,474	4,196	3.7
1985	93,945	2,039	2.2	24,330	1,996	8.2	118,275	4,035	3.4
1986	97,007	1,670	1.7	25,196	1,798	7.1	122,203	3,468	2.8
1987	100,244	1,187	1.2	26,481	1,949	7.4	126,725	3,136	2.5

Source: USTA; adjustments by EMCI, Inc.

lines currently represent approximately 2.5 percent of all lines nationwide.

Multiparty lines are not distributed evenly between Bell companies and the independent companies. In 1987, independent telephone companies had 21 percent of all access lines in the U.S. and over 62 percent of multiparty lines. Multiparty lines currently comprise more than seven percent of all independent company access lines, but only 1.2 percent of BOC access lines.

An interesting subset of these independent companies is those with outstanding loans from the Rural Electrification Administration (REA borrowers). These borrowers represent

Table 6   Multiparty Line Usage by REA Borrowers, 1984-1987 (000s)

Service Type	1984	1985	1986	1987
1 Party				
Business	452	462	471	505
Household	3629	3747	3859	4053
Total	4082	4210	4330	4558
% Change		3	3	5
2 Party				
Business	4	3	3	2
Household	71	59	51	43
Total	75	62	53	45
% Change		-17	-14	-15
4 Party				
Business	10	9	7	6
Household	441	384	321	282
Total	451	393	329	288
% change		-13	-16	-12
8 Party				
Business	7	5	4	3
Household	21	14	10	5
Total	28	19	13	8
% Change		-32	-31	-40
Total Multiparty				
Business	21	16	13	11
Household	532	458	382	330
Total	554	474	395	341
% Change		-14	-17	-14

Source: Underlying data from REA Bulletin Number 300-4, 1984–87.

approximately 20 percent of all access lines operated by inde-. pendent local exchange carriers (LECs). REA borrowers are generally smaller and more rural than other independent LECs. Table 6 indicates the number of multiparty lines owned by REA borrowers from 1984 to 1988.

Figure 7 Total Number of REA Subscribers by Grade

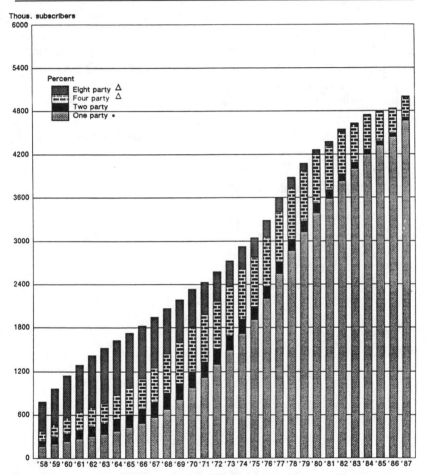

Thous. subscribers

Percent
Eight party △
Four party △
Two party
One party •

'58 '59 '60 '61 '62 '63 '64 '65 '66 '67 '68 '69 '70 '71 '72 '73 '74 '75 '76 '77 '78 '79 '80 '81 '82 '83 '84 '85 '86 '87

☐ Data for 1977 excludes Guam 501 for which complete data was not available.
△ Prior to 1984, four and five party were combined. Beginning in 1984, all grades of service over four party are included in eight party. Service stations (switchers) are also included in eight party. See "Changes in Report" pages 4 and 5 of the 1964 report, for differences in composition of items between 1964 and prior year data.
• Includes pay stations, PBX and Key systems and mobile radiotelephones.

Source: Rural Electrification Administration

As shown across these rural telephone companies, there has been a general decline in the number of multiparty lines—84.5 percent of which are four-party lines—for both businesses and households. Across all multiparty lines, 97 percent serve households, while three percent serve businesses.

The declines in multiparty service, on a percentage basis, have been most dramatic for eight-party lines. This general level of upgrading is most evident when examining Figure 7, which tracks multiparty lines of REA borrowers since 1958. Despite the possible year-to-year variation in the number of REA borrowers, it is evident that eight-party lines have declined dramatically since the 1960s with a corresponding expansion of four-party line usage in the 1970s. Now, four-party lines are being replaced, apparently, by single-party service.

In general, it does not appear that REA borrowers have replaced four-party service with two-party service. In fact, the aggregate number of two-party lines and multiparty business lines has also fallen dramatically since the 1960s.

Regional Variations

To understand how multiparty service varies from one region to another, we divided the country into five regions.

Figure 8 U.S. Regions

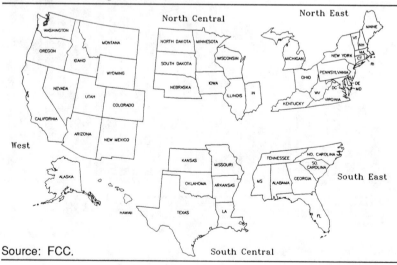

Source: FCC.

The regions, shown in Figure 8, correspond to the regions developed by the FCC for the rural cellular telephone license lotteries, and are used in a number of current studies on rural communications.

As Table 7 shows, multiparty lines operated by REA borrowers are unevenly distributed throughout the United States. The South Central and North East regions together account for

Table 7   Number of Multiparty Lines for REA Borrowers, by
           Region, 1984-87

Year	Number of Borrowers	Exch in Operation	Access Lines (000s)	Multiparty Lines (000s)	Percent Change	% Multi Access
Total U.S.						
1984	946	5,843	4,961	554		11.2
1985	942	5,828	4,913	474	-14.4	9.6
1986	935	5,716	4,964	395	-16.6	8.0
1987	920	5,662	5,171	341	-13.7	6.6
South East						
1984	135	823	1,298	101		7.8
1985	135	811	1,329	81	-19.5	6.1
1986	136	824	1,394	70	-14.1	5.0
1987	135	829	1,470	59	-15.6	4.0
West						
1984	134	809	433	49		11.2
1985	135	825	435	39	-19.6	9.0
1986	132	821	451	32	-16.9	7.2
1987	130	834	452	27	-16.4	6.0
South Central						
1984	171	1,751	1,109	210		19.0
1985	164	1,717	1,130	183	-13.0	16.2
1986	161	1,535	988	137	-25.1	13.9
1987	158	1,507	985	126	-7.8	12.8
North East						
1984	155	765	1,029	158		15.3
1985	158	775	915	142	-9.8	15.6
1986	158	835	1,027	132	-6.9	12.9
1987	153	803	1,150	110	-17.3	9.5
North Central						
1984	351	1,695	1,092	36		3.3
1985	353	1,700	883	28	-21.7	3.2
1986	348	1,701	1,105	24	-17.3	2.1
1987	344	1,689	1,115	19	-19.0	1.7

Source: REA; Calculations by EMCI, Inc.

235,808 multiparty lines, or almost 70 percent of all multiparty lines operated by REA borrowers. The West and North Central regions, by contrast, together only account for 46,183 multiparty lines, only 14 percent of the total.

In aggregate, the total number of multiparty lines reported by REA borrowers declined by 38 percent between 1984 and 1987. Every region except the North East reduced its multiparty lines by at least 40 percent in this period; the North East upgraded 31 percent of its multiparty lines. At the current rate of upgrade, we estimate that multiparty lines will be effectively eliminated from REA borrowers by 1993 (see Figure 9). This is a linear projection that assumes, first, that improvements in technology (such as Basic Exchange Telecommunications Radio Service) will greatly offset the costs of upgrading high-cost multiparty lines in later years. Second, this projection assumes that REA loan programs continue to be available at current rates.

Figure 9   Projections of Multiparty Lines in Use by REA Borrowers, U.S. Total (Percent of Access Lines)

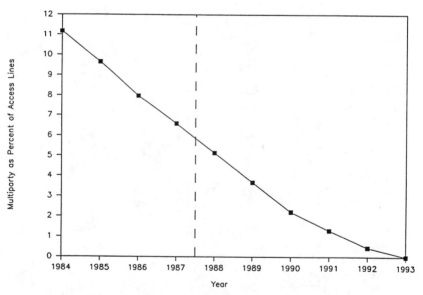

Source: 1984–1987 REA; 1988–1992 EMCI projections based on current regional trends.

While REA borrowers could effectively eliminate multiparty lines by 1993 at current upgrade rates, the five regions are upgrading at different rates (see Figure 10). The North Central region is expected to eliminate multiparty lines first, possibly in the next two years, followed by the South East and the West. Based on current upgrade rates, the North East and South Central regions are expected to be completely upgraded to single-party service in 1992 and 1993, respectively.

Figure 10 Projections of Multiparty Lines in Use by REA Borrowers, Based on Current Upgrade Rates (Percent of Access Lines)

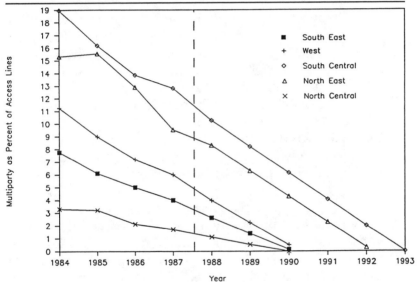

Source: 1984–1987 EMCI calculations from REA data; 1988–1992 EMCI projections.

Bell Operating Companies

Table 5 (above) shows that Bell operating companies (BOCs) operate 79 percent of all access lines and 38 percent of all multiparty lines. Because BOCs generally serve urban areas, multiparty access lines represent less than two percent of total Bell access lines, as opposed to over seven percent for independent telephone companies. The number of BOC multiparty lines in rural areas is not public information.

Like the independents, BOCs have seen a general decline in multiparty line usage. The BOCs have a higher proportion of business establishments using multiparty lines. Based on interviews with Bell operating companies, we believe that a large majority of these BOC multiparty subscribers are actually receiving single-party service on multiparty lines (that is, other users of the lines have upgraded, and thus subscribers may be receiving what amounts to single-party service at grandfathered multiparty rates).

3. Trends in Rural Switching Systems

This chapter focuses primarily on the cost and availability of services; telephone carriers themselves are best equipped to decide which technologies suit their circumstances best. Nevertheless, a large number of important services require digital switching and are generally not available through existing analog telephone switches, although some "digital" services can be made available on some later model stored program control analog switches. Therefore, data on installation of digital switches generally can be used as a surrogate measure for availability of "digital" subscriber services.

REA Borrowers

As with data on multiparty service, the most comprehensive data on digital switching among rural independent LECs comes from the REA. The REA does not directly track the number of analog switches but it does collect data on the number of exchanges and the number of host and remote digital switches. (A host switch contains the subscriber data base and switch logic. Remote switches can be used in conjunction with host switches to reduce switch and cable costs under certain conditions.)

In 1986, the REA estimated that approximately 30 percent of its borrowers' exchanges had been upgraded to digital. These upgraded exchanges serve 45 percent of all REA access lines, since the largest exchanges have been upgraded first. These upgraded exchanges correspond roughly to the number of digital host switches in operation, not counting remote switches connected to hosts. (For this analysis, we used the number of digital hosts reported by REA borrowers as an approximation of the number of digital exchanges in operation.)

Regional Variations in Digital Switching

Nationally, the number of exchanges operated by REA borrowers has declined slightly since 1984 (see Table 8). This is partly due to a consolidation of smaller exchanges. The number of digital exchanges has increased steadily each year, with a corresponding decline in the number of analog exchanges. Approximately 68 percent of all exchanges are currently analog.

Table 8   Switching Equipment Used by REA Borrowers

Year	Number of Borrowers	Exch in Operation	Digital Exch	Analog Exch	Analog % of Exch
Total U.S.					
1984	946	5,843	1,134	4,709	81
1985	942	5,828	1,381	4,447	76
1986	935	5,716	1,560	4,156	73
1987	920	5,662	1,834	3,828	68
South East					
1984	135	823	162	661	80
1985	135	811	189	622	77
1986	136	824	240	584	71
1987	135	829	294	535	65
West					
1984	134	809	289	520	64
1985	135	825	335	490	59
1986	132	821	377	444	54
1987	130	834	432	402	48
South Central					
1984	171	1,751	245	1,506	86
1985	164	1,717	310	1,407	82
1986	161	1,535	304	1,231	80
1987	158	1,507	348	1,159	77
North East					
1984	155	765	149	616	81
1985	158	775	164	611	79
1986	158	835	194	641	77
1987	153	803	218	585	73
North Central					
1984	351	1,695	289	1,406	83
1985	353	1,700	393	1,307	77
1986	348	1,701	445	1,256	74
1987	344	1,689	542	1,147	68

Source: EMCI; Underlying data from REA.

As with multiparty lines, the prevalence of digital switches and the rate of upgrade vary greatly from region to region. The South Central region has the highest percentage of analog exchanges (77 percent), followed by the North East (73 percent analog). REA borrowers in the West have the lowest percent of analog exchanges (48 percent).

At current upgrade rates, the complete replacement of analog switches with digital switches among REA borrowers will not occur until 2016, as Figure 11 shows. Current trends indicate that only the West and South East will be close to completely digital by 1998, as Figure 12 illustrates. The South Central region will not be completely converted until 2013, and the North East region will not be completely converted until 2016.

Figure 11   Projections of Analog Switches in Use by REA Borrowers, U.S. Total (Percent of Exchanges)

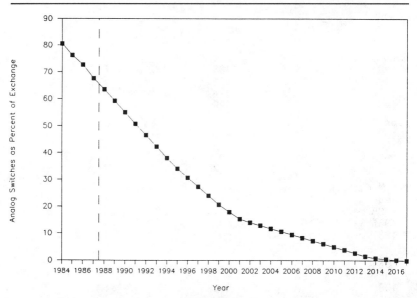

Source: 1984–1987 EMCI calculations from REA data; 1988–2016 EMCI projections.

Other Independent LECs

Most of the large independent LECs are not REA borrowers. According to a recent survey conducted by *Telephony* (Anderson

Figure 12 Projections of Analog Switches in Use by REA Borrowers, Based on Current Trends, by Region (Percent of Exchanges)

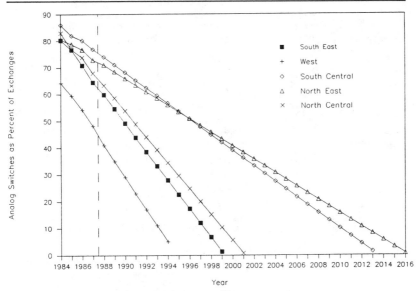

Source: 1984–1987 EMCI calculations from REA data; 1988–2016 EMCI projections.

and Inan, 1989), the top ten independent LECs represented approximately 23 million access lines, approximately 85 percent of all independent access lines. As of June 1988, 61 percent of their lines and 51 percent of their switches were digital (see Table 9). These larger independent LECs thus have a larger percent of digital switches than the REA borrowers, who currently have 32 percent digital switches.

While half of these LEC switches have been upgraded to digital, current capital expenditure plans indicate that the conversion is proceeding rapidly. *Telephony* estimates that the top 18 independents will spend $4.8 billion on their networks in 1989, and that approximately $1.6 billion of this sum will be spent on switching equipment. These companies serve a mix of metropolitan and rural customers. (Data on switching equipment among these LECs based on rural/urban location are not currently available.)

Table 9   Switching Equipment Used by the Top 10 Independent LEDs (June 30, 1988)

	Lines		Switches	
Company	Equipped Lines (000s)*	Equipped Lines % Digital	Local Switches	Local Switches % Digital
GTE	13,445	59.5	2,664	39.5
United	3,884	73.0	1,022	47.0
Contel	2,618	73.2	2,702	67.0
SNET	2,013	33.8	148	38.0
Centel	1,606	82.4	246	51.6
Alltel	1,100	46.0	501	39.0
Cincinnati	929	30.0	58	50.0
Rochester	632	81.0	104	70.0
Century	260	48.9	152	34.4
TDS	267	52.6	209	34.1
Total Ind.	26,754	61.0	7,806	50.6

* Total line capacity (access lines average 85% of equipped lines).

Source: Telephone survey, *Telephony*, January 9, 1989.

Bell Operating Companies

Among the seven regional Bell operating companies, the availability of digital switches varies considerably. According to Anderson and Inan (1989), NYNEX leads the group with 56 percent digital switching. US West and Southwestern Bell have the lowest percent digital, with 21 and 20 percent, respectively. (See Table 10.)

Overall, the RBOCs have converted 34 percent of their switches to digital. This corresponds roughly to the percent of digital switches installed by REA borrowers, but is considerably less than the percent digital installed by the largest independent LECs. *Telephony* reports that of the $14.0 billion of planned network expenditures by the RBOCs, approximately $4.1 billion will be spent on switching equipment in 1989.

As with the large independent LECs, the RBOCs serve a range of metropolitan and rural subscribers. Data are not currently available on the percent of digital switches for BOC rural subscribers.

Table 10   Switching Equipment Used by the Regional Bell Operating Companies (June 30, 1988)

Company	Lines Equipped Lines (000s)*	Equipped Lines % Digital	Switches Local Switches	Local Switches % Digital
Nynex	16,392	38	1,292	56
Bell Atlantic	16,919	35	1,585	39
Bell South	17,515	34	1,323	36
Ameritech	17,594	26	1,262	36
Pacific Telesis	13,900	23	744	33
US West	13,456	22	1,321	21
SW Bell	13,017	18	1,706	20
Total RBOCs	108,793	29	9,233	34

* Total line capacity (access lines average 85% of equipped lines).

Source: Telephone survey, Telephony, January 9, 1989.

4. Additional Cost for Universal Digital Switching by the Year 2000

If the goal of universal access to services made possible by digital switching is adopted by the year 2000, it is clear that intervention must be undertaken to increase the rate of upgrade. Based on current trends, REA borrowers are expected to have a residual of 18 percent analog exchanges in the year 2000. At an upgrade cost of $500 per line (based on digital switches financed by the REA in 1987), this represents an additional investment of approximately $462 million (1987 dollars), or $46.2 million per year for the next 10 years. This amount could be covered by a sustained nine percent real increase of the REA's 1988 total lending authority of $536 million.

As shown in Tables 9 and 10 above, the large independent LECs and the RBOCs also have significant stock of switches to be upgraded to digital. These larger companies face different problems from the REA borrowers and will need incentives to encourage greater investment in digital equipment. (See Chapter Six.)

5. Quality of Transmission

Because businesses are making increasing use of data transmission over telephone lines, the quality of transmission lines is a critical issue. Computer transmission speeds are now typically in the range of 2400 to 9600 bits per second, and some computers communicate at even higher rates. The growing use of facsimile equipment is also increasing the rate of data transmission. These communications technologies cannot tolerate high levels of circuit noise or circuit losses.

The REA recently conducted an analysis of 1,000 local loops, selected at random from REA borrowers (See Table 11). This survey revealed that six percent of all loops experienced unacceptable levels of circuit loss, and seven percent of all loops experienced unacceptable levels of circuit noise. Because there was little overlap between the two deficiencies, approximately 10 to 12 percent of REA lines are shown to have failed REA circuit objectives. However, only approximately three percent of these circuits had deficiencies considered to be service affecting by the

Table 11 Summary of Local Loops with Transmission Deficiencies, based on 1,000 Loop Survey REA Borrowers, 1986

Measurement	Number of Loops	Percent Loops
A. Circuit Loss (dB)		
8.1 - 9.0	33	3.3
9.1 - 10.0	14	1.4
10.0+	9	.9
Total over 8.0 dB	56	5.6
Total considered service affecting	9	.9
B. Circuit Noise (dBrnc)		
21 - 26	43	4.3
27 - 30	14	1.4
30+	8	.8
Total over 20 dBrnc	65	6.5
Total considered service affecting	22	2.2

Note: The REA maximum circuit loss objective is 8 dB. The maximum circuit noise objective is 20 dBrnc. Circuit loss of over 10 dB and circuit noise of over 26 dBrnc are considered service affecting.

Source: 1986 REA Loop Survey

REA. It is believed that there are a significant number of other independent LEC and BOC lines in rural areas with transmission deficiencies.

6. Mobile Cellular Systems

One relatively new communications technology with great potential is cellular mobile telephone. This technology has been extremely popular in metropolitan areas. Since its inception in 1984, cellular has grown to 1.6 million subscribers by mid-1988. The licensing process for rural areas began in 1988, and the first rural cellular operations can be expected to come on line in 1990.

While all rural areas will soon be licensed for cellular, it is unlikely that all rural areas will have service, at least over the next five years. The cellular industry is characterized by high fixed costs that are somewhat independent of market size. As a result, the fixed costs to build in small markets may be too high to make a profit given the small potential demand.

In its 1988 report *The Demand for Cellular Telephone Service in Rural Service Areas*, EMCI forecast the demand for cellular in all of the FCC-defined rural service areas (RSAs). The report projects the likely subscriber demand that would exist if RSAs exemplified the same relative intensity of demand as metropolitan areas, by year of operation. Additionally, the report takes account of "roaming demand," that is, demand for cellular telephone service from subscribers who do not reside within the market.

Four percent of the RSA markets are projected to have at least 3,000 subscribers in year five (see Figure 13). This is roughly comparable to demand projections for small metropolitan markets. While the level of demand is comparable, the markets may not have equal economic value due to differences in population and business density, topography, and roaming demand potential.

The majority of RSA markets have much lower levels of projected demand. Sixty percent of all RSA markets are projected to have a subscriber base of less than 1,500 in year five. Thirty-seven percent of RSA markets are very small markets, with projected fifth year demand of less than 1,000.

Figure 13   Distribution of Rural Cellular Markets by Projected Number of Fifth Year Subscribers (Percent of Markets)

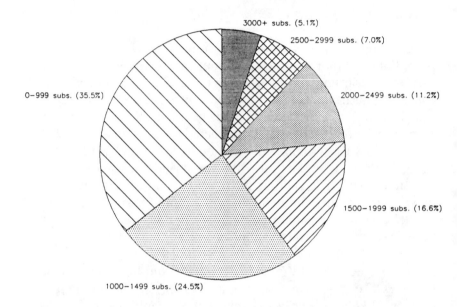

3000+ subs. (5.1%)

2500–2999 subs. (7.0%)

2000–2499 subs. (11.2%)

0–999 subs. (35.5%)

1500–1999 subs. (16.6%)

1000–1499 subs. (24.5%)

Source: EMCI, Inc.

EMCI determined that at least one operating system can be expected to be built in almost all markets with 1,500 or more fifth year subscribers. These markets usually have sufficient concentrations of demand within the RSA to permit at least break-even operations. The larger RSAs (based on subscriber projections) also tend to be the RSAs with higher roaming demand potential, as shown in Figure 14. For example, many rural markets will be financially viable because they have major interstate highways passing through them.

The demand from this "roaming" traffic may justify the construction of a cellular system even if the demand within the market is very small. This additional demand will be sufficient to make many marginal markets feasible. Somewhat smaller

Figure 14 Roaming Demand Indicators by Market Size, All Rural Cellular Markets

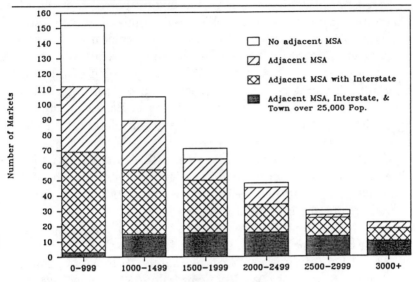

Source: EMCI, Inc.   Projected Fifth Year Subscribers

markets, with as few as 1200 projected fifth year subscribers, will also likely be feasible RSA markets for at least one operator, provided that they have high roaming demand potential.

Based on this analysis, it is likely that approximately 60 percent of all RSA markets will be constructed by at least one operator. These markets will cover a much higher percentage of households, since the rural areas with relatively higher population density will be built first.

7. Summary

The general condition of rural telecommunications is somewhat encouraging. While there are areas requiring investment at rates higher than we are currently experiencing, all indicators show that current investments are improving existing services and providing new services. The rate of upgrade, however, may not be able to keep up with even more rapid advances in urban areas.

Universal access. This is still a problem in rural areas. The primary reason for households without service is poverty. A secondary reason, affecting a much smaller number of households without telephones, is geographical remoteness. Increased subsidies and/or wider availability of lifeline service are necessary to make significant increases in telephone penetration rates.

Single-party telephone service. While 7.4 percent of all independent telephone company access lines are multiparty, these lines are being upgraded at a steady pace. Based on current upgrade rates, REA borrowers will have completely upgraded to single-party service by 1993.

Digital switching. It is unlikely that REA borrowers will be able to complete the conversion to digital switches by the year 2000 without additional assistance. A major effort will be required to ensure universal digital service by the end of the century, including those areas served by BOCs and larger independent telephone companies.

Quality of transmission. Approximately 10 to 12 percent of local loops tested by the REA were below REA objectives for background noise or circuit loss. Approximately three percent of local loops had deficiencies determined to be service affecting. Because of the high priority placed on data communications by today's businesses, low transmission quality may inhibit business growth.

Mobile cellular. While cellular has been restricted to metropolitan areas until now, the licensing process will permit rural cellular by 1990. It is likely that approximately 60 percent of all rural cellular markets will be viable for at least one carrier. These markets will cover considerably more than 60 percent of the rural population. Additional markets are likely to come on line over time should technology improvements continue to reduce the fixed investment required to offer this service.

SIX

TOWARD THE YEAR 2000:
POLICY GOALS AND
RECOMMENDATIONS

The long-standing goal of "universal service," that is, making voice telephone service accessible to all U.S. households, has been nearly attained. Since the 1940s, the REA has been the government's chief vehicle for implementing universal service through its loans to rural telephone carriers. In the process, as reported in Chapter Three, above, the Gross Domestic Product (GDP) has increased six to seven times more than the government invested, via interest rate subsidies. Because of this long-term investment, private businesses have thrived, rural residents have enjoyed many social amenities, and rural regions have been able to enjoy brighter economic prospects.

It is time to reassess whether the goal of telephone service for all is sufficient in our new economic and technological environment. Times have changed since the early policymakers made their commitment to universal service. Rural economies have undergone wrenching declines as the national and global economies create more service-based and information-intensive businesses. The telecommunications industry itself has blossomed into a dynamic, innovative sector of the economy, transforming the routine practices of American business.

Amidst all this change, rural telecommunications policy has not kept pace. In particular, it is no longer responsive to the contemporary economic needs of rural America. This is a costly shortcoming, because the absence of adequate telecommunications is a major structural barrier to economic expansion in many rural communities. After the breakup of AT&T and the advent of new FCC telecommunications policies, people in rural areas tended to oppose the changes. Now most people realize that, like it or not, the old telecommunications industry structure is gone forever. Most also realize that the rural economy's problems are structural, not cyclical.

It is clearly time to revisit and reformulate the goals for rural telecommunications policy. The economic future of rural America is at stake.

The National Telecommunications and Information Agency (NTIA), a part of the U.S. Department of Commerce, recently issued the first comprehensive executive branch review of the communication and information sectors in 20 years. The report, *Telecom 2000, Charting the Course for a New Century*, published in October 1988, recommends that between now and the year 2000 the U.S. should invest in the telecommunications infrastructure needed to achieve "universal information service." This goal updates the prior goal of universal voice telephone service to include access to other important information services.

The Telecom 2000 report made the following general recommendations:

- "Policies should be adopted which will make it possible to achieve access to 'universal information service' whereby ordinary small business and residential telephone subscribers have full access to the wealth of information and other innovative services upon which our success as an economy and society is coming to depend.
- "More than this, we must focus on the creation of the world's best telecommunications and information infrastructure, which could lead to the availability of 'video dial tone' and other innovative services.
- "More reliance on competitive marketplace forces and incentives is needed, and barriers to competition, including in local exchange and cable services, should be removed.

- "Rates for competitive services must be economically deregulated and rates for noncompetitive services moved toward cost, so that the marketplace will make the investments necessary to develop an advanced telecommunications and information infrastructure.
- "Policies for assistance to low-income users should be focused, in orders to target assistance directly to those who otherwise might be precluded. Market failure, moreover, should not be assumed in the case of additional communications offerings. If it materializes, which is unlikely, steps can then be taken to ensure access to new services deemed vital."

The NTIA report devoted a separate chapter to the topic "Ensuring Services for Rural America," concluding with a series of specific rural telecommunications policy recommendations:

- "Ensure that policies take fully into account the different circumstances prevailing in rural and urban America.
- "Promote maximum competition generally, but assess each competitive policy as to its potential to be counter productive in sparsely populated areas where the economic base may not be sufficient to support a single firm, much less competing firms.
- "Continue existing support programs as needed and desirable, to ease the transition to a more competitive communications environment overall, without placing a disproportionate cost burden on rural residents.
- "Pursue policies which encourage telephone companies, including the Bell companies, to offer new services in rural areas.
- "Efforts to attract industry to rural areas should include consideration of enhancing the telecommunications and information facilities and services available through links with fiber optic or microwave networks, or teleports, for example.
- "Encourage telecommunications companies and organizations to assist in economic development, and to provide training and technical assistance to small independent telephone companies."

We endorse these general recommendations but wish to elaborate further. As the NTIA report made clear, the general goal of a competitive telecommunications marketplace needs to be tempered by the addition of special policies for rural areas because a policy of competition could be counter productive in sparsely populated areas where the economic base may not be sufficient to support even a single firm. Small rural telephone companies have local service franchise obligations to serve all the people in their franchise area. This service obligation was undertaken in exchange for assurances that competitors would not be allowed to "cream skim" the more attractive parts of the franchises, such as the towns, leaving the rural countryside unserved. The following sections offer more specific goals and recommendations by which rural telecommunications policy can enhance rural development.

1. Rural Telecommunications Policy Goals

As discussed in Chapter One, there are three primary reasons for government intervention in rural telecommunications policy at this time:

- To achieve improved economic performance in rural areas by providing a basic infrastructure needed for development;
- To help rural America adjust to the new telecommunications marketplace by way of special transition policies; and
- To empower rural communities with an equal opportunity to participate in the national economy and determine their own destiny.

Advances in technology have precipitated recent regulatory changes, which in turn are intended to facilitate innovation, competition and quality products and services. For that reason, the authors of this report conclude that it would be a serious policy mistake for government to dictate which technologies are best for any group of business or residential consumers. Instead, we focus on the generic telecommunications services that are most critical to rural economic development and how government can provide incentives that encourage these services in the most cost-effective way possible.

Based on the evidence and analysis of the preceding chapters, a general policy goal can be stated:

Encourage rural telephone carriers to provide affordable access to telecommunications and information services comparable to those available in urban areas.

A more sophisticated infrastructure of rural telecommunications services is needed if economic development is to take place. Creating opportunities for rural residents and businesses to purchase modern telecommunications services at affordable prices does not mean a government-funded entitlement program. It means devising a system of incentives, a pool of loan funds, and technical assistance so that the private sector can do the job.

The assistance and incentive structure should be designed to provide, by the year 2000, affordable "universal information service" to all rural residents and businesses. More specifically, "affordable access to telecommunications and information services" implies ten goals:

1. *Make voice telephone service available to everyone.*

The current policy goal of universal service should be retained in order to reach the remaining households that do not have access to, or cannot afford, basic telephone service.

2. *Make single-party access to the public switched telephone network available to everyone.*

Multiparty lines, still the norm in some rural areas, cannot accommodate computer modems, facsimile machines and other modern telecommunications facilities. Rural economic development requires access to single-party telephone lines.

3. *Improve the quality of telephone service sufficiently to allow rapid and reliable transmission of facsimile documents and data.*

Participation in the modern U.S. economy requires reliable, rapid and economical document and data transmission. Yet many rural telephone lines are of poor quality, which slows down transmission speed or requires multiple transmissions to correct errors. In either case, the rural user pays more for the longer connect time. Upgrading substandard rural lines is a key challenge for rural telecommunications policy.

4. *Provide rural telephone users with equal access to competitive long-distance carriers.*

Most urban subscribers can choose among several long-distance telephone companies; most rural subscribers have a single monopoly carrier. If rural residents are to enjoy the fruits of the competitive U.S. long-distance telephone policy, rural carriers must upgrade their equipment to provide equal access to long-distance companies.

5. *Provide rural telephone users with local access to value-added data networks.*

Most urban telephone subscribers can access value-added data networks such as Telenet and Tymnet ("enhanced service providers," in FCC parlance) with a local call. Once subscribers are connected to the value-added network, they can reach a wide variety of digital information services without paying long-distance rates. Most rural subscribers cannot reach information services without first calling a value-added network in the nearest large city via a long-distance call.

6. *Provide 911 emergency service with automatic number identification in rural areas.*

In urban areas, 911 emergency service has become an integral part of fire, health and public safety services. Newer 911 telephone services can provide automatic identification of the calling number. When connected to a computerized database, the calling number can be used to identify the location of the calling telephone—which can then help 911 dispatchers send the right services to the right location immediately. Automatic number identification may be even more important in rural areas than in urban areas because dispatchers may be many miles away from the calling party and may not know the local geography or which rural emergency service jurisdiction should help the caller.

7. *Expand mobile (cellular) telephone service.*

Given the greater distances and time spent traveling in rural areas, mobile telephone service has many obvious benefits. It can be useful to individual businesses and especially to rural transportation services. In areas not served by cellular telephone services, radio telephone technology may be a feasible alternative.

8. *Make available touch tone and custom calling services, including such services as three-way calling, call forwarding and call waiting.*

Touch tone service, a rarity in many rural areas, is a prerequisite for a variety of business information services such as telephone banking, telephone-assisted reservations, and information access services. While custom calling services may provide only a minor convenience for personal users, it has become a significant productivity tool in business. To make possible these new services, many analog switches in rural telephones must be replaced with digital switches.

9. *Make voice messaging services available via local phone calls.*

Telephone answering machines have become a necessity for many small businesses and busy residences. Good quality touch tone telephone access may be necessary to use some of the helpful features, such as calling in for your messages when out of the office. Some larger companies have begun using "voicemail" services with features not available on individual answering machines, including shared "mailboxes," broadcast or narrowcast messaging, storage, routing and retrieval of voice messages and automated replies to incoming messages. In the near future, a number of urban telephone companies will be offering small businesses and residential subscribers voice messaging services previously available only in large companies. It may be desirable for rural telephone carriers to include voice messaging as a service offering or to provide gateways to third-party voice messaging services.

10. *Enable rural telephone carriers to provide the telecommunications and information services that become generally available in urban areas.*

In the more competitive information services environment, many new services are likely to become available, including video information services via cable television. Any policies and regulations adopted in furtherance of the first nine services in this list should not be written so narrowly as to inhibit other services that may become available in the next few years.

To achieve the goal of universal information service by the year 2000, as defined by the ten goals above, will require specific initiatives by the federal government, state governments and the private sector. These ten goals were intended to enumerate the major telecommunications services useful for economic development that are or soon will be generally available in urban areas. As indicated in the tenth goal, the specific list may change, but the general intent is to narrow the gap between rural and urban service availability. The policy actions required to achieve these goals are discussed below.

2. Recommended Changes In Federal Policies

Rural Electrification Administration
Recommendation 1:
Congress should update and expand the REA's mission to include fostering affordable rural access to the basic communications tools of the Information Age. Specifically, the REA should be mandated to provide loan funds and technical assistance to authorized rural carriers in

order to make available to rural residents and businesses all of the telecommunications services that are generally available in urban areas.

Recommendation 2:
Congress should increase the REA's lending authority by about 30 percent (approximately $150 million per year) to accelerate the conversion from analog to digital telephone switches in rural America and to help provide rural residents with access to voice, data, video and mobile services comparable to those available to urban residents.

The REA telephone program is one of the great unsung success stories in rural economic development. At relatively minor cost to taxpayers in the form of interest subsidies, this program has helped build the rural telephone infrastructure which has fostered rural development over the past 50 years. REA staff know the problems and opportunities of rural telecommunications and are respected by the rural telephone industry. A modest expansion of this existing, successful program is the most cost-effective way to achieve the policy goals enumerated above.

The most important policy action required to achieve the larger goal of universal information service access is to broaden the mandate and expand the funding of the REA telephone program. Funding and technical assistance should not be limited to the narrow goal of universal basic voice telephone service. Funds and technical assistance should continue to be made available for conversion of multiparty lines to single-party lines, upgrade of analog switches to digital switches, upgrade of line quality and otherwise adding the telephone facilities necessary to make rural telephone service comparable to the quality and variety of urban service. Although already implicit in existing REA authority, it would be helpful to grant explicit authority to provide funds and technical assistance for radio telephone, satellite and other technologies, in addition to conventional wireline technology, that may be appropriate to complete the basic universal voice telephone service mission at affordable costs. Further, the REA should be authorized to provide loan funds and technical assistance to help rural carriers interconnect with long-distance voice and value-added carriers, and provide voice, data, and video information, and mobile telephone services.

Funding levels for REA loans and loan guarantee programs should be increased to accommodate this expanded mission. We estimate that a nine or ten percent increase in funding authority would be sufficient to complete the conversion of REA telephone carrier switches from analog to digital by the year 2000. (See Chapter Five.) This translates into an additional $50 million of loans and loan guarantee authority per year for ten years.

Since these are loans and loan guarantees rather than grants, the cost to the federal government (and therefore to taxpayers) is limited to the amount of the interest rate subsidy involved. For example, if the government were paying an average interest rate of seven percent to borrow money, and REA borrowers were paying six percent, the one percent interest rate subsidy would cost taxpayers $500,000 per year for an outstanding loan balance of $50 million. (This example assumes that some of the funds would continue to be loaned at the subsidized five percent rate and that other funds would continue to be loaned at the Rural Telephone Bank's cost of funds rate.)

The REA would also need additional lending authority in order to finance equipment needed to provide the full range of telecommunications services generally available in urban areas. With about 20 percent of the funding now committed to the traditional telephone loan program—or increased annual lending authority of about $100 million—the REA should be able to undertake this broader mission. As the amount of funds needed to attain universal voice telephone service declines, the REA should have authority to adjust the proportion of the total funds allocated to video, data and cellular equipment.

Any proposal to increase government spending obviously must be scrutinized in the light of federal budget deficits. If necessary, REA loans for a broader telecommunications mission could be made at the Rural Telephone Bank cost of funds rate or the Federal Financing Bank cost of funds rate. Subsidized interest rate funds are, of course, preferable because they make it more likely that rural development goals will be achieved by the year 2000. Nevertheless, major progress could be achieved without interest rate subsidy just by making additional capital funds available and by making the necessary technical assistance available through the REA.

Federal Communications Commission

Recommendation 3:

The FCC should continue its support of rural telecommunications by maintaining nationwide long distance average rate schedules. It should also continue to authorize "lifeline" and "universal service" funds out of interstate long-distance revenues. It should encourage the expansion of competitive long-distance services by permitting local exchange carriers to initiate upgrades to equal access facilities.

Recommendation 4:

The FCC should encourage the development of video and other information services in rural areas by broadening the waiver of cable television and telephone cross-ownership restrictions in rural areas.

Recommendation 5:

The FCC should offer incentives for the Bell operating companies and larger independent telephone companies to prepare and implement plans to upgrade completely their rural facilities by the year 2000 to provide their rural service areas all telecommunications services generally available in urban service areas.

FCC regulatory policies to date have generally supported rural telecommunications interests. In particular, the nationwide averaging policy for long-distance rates and the support for "universal service," "lifeline" and "Link Up America" programs have helped keep telephone service accessible and affordable. These programs and policies should be continued.

Still, new FCC initiatives could help improve rural telecommunications further. For example, the FCC should permit local exchange carriers to upgrade their switching facilities to provide equal access to competitive long-distance carriers. Currently, local exchange carriers must wait until a request for such an upgrade is received from a long-distance carrier.

In order to stimulate expansion of cable television and other video services into rural areas, the FCC should expand the current waiver of the telephone-cable television cross-ownership prohibition for rural telephone carriers (or alternately, remove the prohibition altogether).

In addition, the FCC should encourage the BOCs and larger independent telephone companies to install by the year 2000, facilities suitable to provide to all customers in their rural service areas telecommunications comparable to those provided in their urban service areas.

The FCC should also set appropriate minimum quality standards for local and long-distance access lines (especially those connecting independent rural carriers to the national telephone network), and require larger carriers to meet these standards by the year 2000. The FCC should establish the availability and quality of services that carriers must meet if they elect to convert to price caps as an alternative to rate of return regulation. Under price cap regulation, it is necessary to regulate quality of service in any event. These service quality obligations could be included as additional requirements to be met in the event that carriers elect price cap regulation.

Statistics for rural areas served by BOCs and larger independent companies are not as readily available as the statistics for areas served by REA carriers. Nevertheless, the data on BOC digital switches presented in Chapter Five above suggest that digital capability is available at levels comparable to those found among small REA-supported rural carriers. Since major urban areas served by BOCs have already been upgraded, it may be reasonable to infer that rural areas served by BOCs, on the average, lag behind the smaller REA-funded carriers and the larger independent telephone companies, although some of the BOC switches may be late model stored program control analog switches that do provide many of the services usually provided through digital switches. The BOCs and largest independent telephone companies do not need REA loan funds or technical assistance to upgrade their rural services. FCC regulation may be the most practical way to encourage these larger companies to upgrade their facilities.

Justice Department
Recommendation 6:

> The Justice Department should recommend to Judge Harold Greene, in connection with the AT&T consent decree, that the BOCs be given waivers or other incentives sufficient to induce them to provide infrastructure and gateways for information services in their rural areas comparable to those available in urban areas.

In order for FCC waivers of telephone and cable television cross-ownership restrictions to apply to the BOCs as well as other rural telephone carriers, additional court approval may be required. Comparable special arrangements may also need to be made for data and voice services to sparsely populated rural areas where it may be difficult to attract even a single enhanced service provider and nearly impossible to attract multiple enhanced service competitors. This recommendation assumes that the FCC will condition all authority for telephone companies to offer enhanced services on compliance with an FCC-approved Open Network Architecture (ONA) standard that permits all information and enhanced service providers to access the network transmission facilities of the telephone carrier on the same basis as the enhanced services offered by the telephone carrier.

Rural Development Programs
Recommendation 7:

> All federal agencies involved in rural development programs should include telecommunications planning and coordination and authorize funding for telecommunications services as part of their programs.

All federal economic and social development programs for rural areas—whether administered by the Departments of Agriculture, Commerce, Education, Health and Human Services, Interior or Justice—should consider the essential role of telecommunications in their policy planning. For example, the provision of enhanced 911 emergency services for rural areas may be even more critical than for urban areas. Similarly, computers used in rural health or education programs may require reliable data communication links. Rural schools may need video services by cable or satellite to provide specialized instruction. Rural health clinics may need telecommunications for medical diagnosis, monitoring and continuing education. Federal agencies pursuing pilot projects, demonstrations and ongoing rural economic or social development programs should work with the appropriate telecommunications carriers to provide the necessary linkages.

3. Recommended Changes In State Policies

Public Utility Commissions
Recommendation 8:
> State PUCs should encourage telephone carriers to offer new information services by permitting accelerated cost recovery accounting on obsolete equipment not suitable for modern services.

State Public Utility Commissions (PUCs) that have not accepted the FCC depreciation schedules should change their depreciation accounting rules. Currently, in some states, carriers can recover their original investment in capital equipment from subscriber charges only if the equipment is kept in service for the entire extended depreciation accounting period. This discourages carriers from improving their equipment or services. REA loans to upgrade rural telephone facilities would not achieve their intended purpose if state PUC policies inhibit the replacement of obsolete facilities. To advance the federal policies recommended above, PUCs should remove regulatory barriers that prevent regulated rural telephone carriers from improving service quality or offering new information services beyond voice telephone service.

State Development Agencies
Recommendation 9:

    State development and social service agencies should include telecommunications issues within their planning agendas, and should request their PUC to remove any state regulations that inhibit deployment of new telecommunications facilities appropriate for rural development.

The rationale for recommendation 7 above is even more relevant for state economic development programs because state governments typically play a large role in state economic development. Also, many social services such as education are primarily state, not federal, responsibilities. It is therefore important that state government programs for rural economic or social development coordinate their work with appropriate telecommunications carriers.

    State PUCs and state economic development agencies traditionally have little to do with each other, often resulting in policies that work at cross purposes. To deal with this problem, state economic development agencies should review telephone regulations and ask the state PUC to eliminate any regulations that needlessly stymie the improvement of telecommunications facilities and services.

Policy Coordination
Recommendation 10:

    State governments that have not already done so should establish a centralized telecommunications policy office to assist all state agencies in telecommunications planning and to help coordinate policy among various state agencies, including the PUC.

As telecommunications and information services become more important to social and economic development, state governments need greater expertise in these areas. A specially designated office in state government could help diverse state agencies navigate the complexities of telecommunications technology, policy and law, to ensure that state telecommunications policies and programs are better coordinated.

4. Carrier Initiatives

Local exchange carriers are essential to the achievement of universal information service. The rural carriers, including BOCs with operations in or connections to rural areas, should endorse the goal of universal information service, and develop their own initiatives to advance that goal by the year 2000. Organizations such as the U.S. Telephone Association (USTA), National Telephone Cooperative Association (NCTA), the Organization for the Protection and Advancement of Small Telephone Companies (OPASTCO), National Rural Telecom Association (NRTA), and National Rural Electric Cooperative Association (NRECA) as well as state telephone associations, should help develop new initiatives and policies to achieve this goal.

5. Further Studies

Policymakers never seem to have as much evidence as they would like to support the decisions they are asked to make. But at some point, policymakers have to make their best judgment and get on with the decision. Enough evidence is already available to justify moving ahead with the preceding policy recommendations. Suggestions for further research or policy analyses should not be used as an excuse to avoid or delay implementing the policies outlined above. It would be unnecessary or unfair to hold rural telecommunications policies to a higher standard of evidence than is typically required for policy initiatives in other areas.

That said, several additional studies could help clarify some unresolved issues. Such studies would be particularly useful if they could be completed soon enough to contribute to the current dialogue about telecommunications for rural development.

Technology and Cost Studies

What are the costs, availability, type and quality of telecommunications services currently available in rural and urban areas? It would be helpful to the policy debate to extend the analysis set forth in Chapter Five above, especially if data could be provided on a state-by-state instead of a regional basis. Because most of the information in Chapter Five came from the REA, it would be useful to obtain more information about the rural areas served by the BOCs and independent carriers that are not REA borrowers. Such information could help refine the calculations of the actual investments needed to achieve universal information service by the year 2000. It could also help determine what government regulations, loans, loan guarantees and technical assistance would be required to meet that goal.

To promote better rural telephone service, it would also be helpful to evaluate the costs and benefits of satellite, radio and other technical alternatives to conventional wireline telephone.

Studies of Economic Benefits

Rural economic development initiatives could proceed with greater confidence if there were more detailed studies of rural business needs and the economic benefits of enhanced telecommunications. It would be useful to have a review and summary of the many studies that have been conducted on how businesses (service and information businesses in particular) choose to locate where they do. Since opportunities for rural business development will be more plentiful in information- and service-related ventures than in manufacturing over the next decade, this sort of research could be useful to rural planners.

Comparative Studies

There are several international initiatives that might have relevance for U.S. rural telecommunications and economic development policy. In Scandinavia, a number of "telecottages" have been established in rural areas to provide access to facsimile machines, data networks and personal computers. The European Economic Community, too, has a program to enhance rural telecommunications and information services. Although foreign experiences cannot be transferred directly to the United States, comparative analyses of appropriate foreign telecommunications innovations could yield important lessons for American planners and policymakers.

Demonstration and Pilot Projects

Pilot or demonstration projects can often reveal more about promising new technologies or services than theoretical studies. The Iowa shared network switch for equal access to competitive long-distance services, for example, could add access to value-added data networks such as Telenet and Tymnet; rural residents could then reach a variety of information services with a local call. By evaluating usage patterns and benefits resulting from such pilot projects, other rural areas could better plan future telecommunications projects.

Information Dissemination

There is a need to disseminate more widely the research that already exists about how telecommunications and information services can stimulate rural economic development. Information about the successes, failures and new experiments should also be made available to businesses, service agencies, and rural residents.

State Policy Analysis

Most rural development programs are administered through state governments (even when financed by federal funds) and state telecommunications policies can have a substantial impact on the rural economy. It makes sense to give closer scrutiny to the interaction of telecommunications policy and rural development policy at the state level. A study of the policy issues raised by this report in the specific factual context of one or two states might expose additional problems and issues that cannot be explored in a necessarily more general national study such as this one. A state-level study could provide a useful model for state-initiated rural development projects. Such a study is urgently needed because much of what happens in rural development over the next decade will happen at the state, not the federal, level.

Such a state-level study of telecommunications policy for rural development should include the same facets that were examined in the present study, but with more emphasis on the specific rural development activities underway in that state. It should include a survey of the current level of rural telecommunications facilities, a survey of the telecommunications industry structure, the relevant policies of the state Public Utilities Commission, and a review of the various rural development programs and activities that could utilize rural telecommunications services.

6. Conclusion

The most striking aspect of the importance of telecommunications services to rural development is its pervasiveness. An adequate rural telecommunications infrastructure is critical to all types of rural business activities, including agriculture and manufacturing, and is particularly critical for the service sector, where most new job growth is expected to occur. An adequate telecommunications infrastructure is similarly critical to social services in rural communities. We don't know any other way to reduce the common barrier that is the defining characteristic of rural communities—distance.

In the past, it has been tempting to describe rural America as too diverse for a rural development policy to be effective. Indeed, a rural development policy targeted only at agriculture, manufacturing, tourism or almost any other specific sector would leave most of rural America untouched. Telecommunications is a clear exception. Development of an adequate telecommunications infrastructure will have important benefits for all regions and virtually all rural activities.

In a simpler, earlier era, universal basic voice telephone service was an ambitious yet appropriate telecommunications policy goal. Now rural needs are more complex. What is needed is "universal information service"—affordable access to a wide variety of telecommunications services. Rural businesses and residents need single-party access to the switched telephone network, high-quality transmission lines for reliable facsimile document and data transmission, equal access to competitive long-distance carriers, local access to value-added data networks, mobile telephone service, and other new communications and information services.

In the long run, the success of a telecommunications-based rural development policy will depend on how rural residents and entrepreneurs in different regions with different development strategies actually use the specific technologies. Given the rich economic and social returns that have already been demonstrated, however, we believe that new investments in telecommunications are a promising strategy for rejuvenating rural America. The economic and social returns far outweigh the comparatively modest investment required.

U.S. RURAL TELECOMMUNICATIONS: THE PLAYERS

1. The Local Telephone Carriers

The heart of rural telecommunications is the local telephone companies and cooperatives, usually called local exchange carriers (LECs). These carriers provide local telephone service and provide for their local customers interconnection to one or more long-distance telephone carriers. Most often the long-distance carrier that rural LECs connect with is American Telephone and Telegraph (AT&T), either directly or through the nearest Bell operating company (BOC).

At the outset of 1989 there were approximately 1400 LECs in the U.S., including 22 BOCs organized into seven regional Bell operating companies (RBOCs). The RBOCs were created in 1984 as a result of the court-ordered AT&T consent decree divesting AT&T of its local telephone operations. Although most of the territory of the BOCs is urban, a number of rural areas are included.

The Bell companies serve about 80 percent of the approximately 84 million U.S. telephone households. Most rural areas, however, are served by "independent" (that is, non-Bell) telephone carriers, which serve the remaining 20 percent of U.S. telephone households. The largest independent telephone holding company, General Telephone and Electronics (GTE), alone serves eight percent of the telephone households. The next largest independent telephone companies, United Telecommunications and Contel, together serve about four percent of the telephone households, leaving eight percent for the more than 1300 other telephone carriers.

Most of the local telephone carriers are quite small. For example, the Volcano Telephone Company of Pine Grove, California, ranked 150th in size, has 7214 customer lines (called subscriber access lines). More than 1200 carriers are even smaller. Island Telephone Company, for example, serving a tiny island off the coast of Bangor, Maine, has 34 subscribers.

These small telephone carriers were organized, many of them as non-profit cooperatives, to provide essential telecommunication services to their communities and rural territories. Both small and large companies are dedicated to keeping telephone service operating for their subscribers. Some have access to commercial financing for the substantial costs of a capital-intensive utility business; many do not. Some have sophisticated understanding of the rapid changes going on in telecommunications and information technology, including digital switches, fiber optics, satellites, and new radio telephone technology, but many do not. Some have sophisticated understanding of the rapidly changing regulatory environment as the industry adjusts to a more competitive and differently regulated policy environment; many do not. Some have financial officers who understand the nuances of the new telephone carrier accounting rules recently ordered by the Federal Communications Commission (FCC); others may have bookkeepers who may not understand clearly how the old or the new accounting rules differ from generally accepted accounting principles (GAAP), as used by other industries.

2. The Associations

Given the wide diversity evident in the 1400 local telephone carriers, it should be no surprise that there are a number of different associations serving the interests of the industry.

NECA

The National Exchange Carriers Association (NECA) is the financial clearinghouse distributing the revenues collected from long-distance telephone calls that are allocated to cover the local switching and access line costs associated with long-distance calls.

Every long-distance call in the U.S. involves two local exchanges and access lines connecting the calling and the called parties to those exchanges, as well as the long-distance lines and switches in between. All long distance carriers must pay to each of the local carriers involved a portion of the revenue they receive from each long-distance telephone call, to cover the local costs at each end. Rather than account for every call separately, the revenues and the associated costs are "pooled", with NECA administering the "pools" of costs and revenues, and allocating the funds as agreed among the carriers in accordance with FCC regulations.

The prices for interstate long-distance calls are set based on the distance between the two locations, independently of the actual costs associated with the particular locations involved. The costs of connecting a call from Washington, DC, to New York City may be less than the costs of connecting a call of similar distance between two rural locations because the larger the volume of traffic on each route, the lower the cost per call. The charges the long-distance carriers pay for access to the local exchange facilities are paid into the pools administered by NECA, which pays them out to the local carriers based on their costs, but subject to a cap set by the FCC.

For particularly high-cost rural areas there is a "universal service" fund administered by NECA using a portion of the revenue from all long-distance calls. NECA files tariffs at the FCC for the access charges long-distance carriers pay to the local carriers (except for some carriers who file their own directly), with the total price sufficient to recover total interstate costs, even though the price for a particular call may have no connection to the actual cost for that particular call.

(NECA is located at 100 South Jefferson Road, Whippany, NJ 07981, telephone (201) 884-8000. Bruce W. Baldwin is President and Chief Operating Officer.)

NRECA

The National Rural Electric Cooperative Association (NRECA) is, as the name implies, the organization of the nation's rural electric cooperatives. It is particularly concerned with the rural electrification programs of the REA, which are larger than the REA telephone programs. Recently, it has been active in supporting electric cooperatives to provide telecommunications services by communications satellite networks, particularly video for their rural subscribers, and data services for their member systems.

(NRECA is located at 1800 Massachusetts Ave. N.W., Washington DC 20036, telephone (202) 857-9500. Bob Bergland is the Executive Vice President.)

NRTA

The National Rural Telecom Association has represented the interests of commercial REA telephone borrowers in Washington for almost 30 years. The association concentrates its activities on preserving the telephone lending programs of the Rural Electrification Administration as viable sources of financing for rural telephone companies at reasonable rates of interest.

(NRTA is located at 1455 Pennsylvania Ave., N.W. Suite 1200, Washington, DC 20004, telephone (202) 628-0210. John F. O'Neal is general counsel of the organization.)

NRTC

The National Rural Telecommunications Cooperative was organized in 1986 through the combined efforts of NRECA and the National Rural Utilities Cooperative Finance Corporation, an organization that had previously been concerned primarily with rural electric cooperatives. NRTC is also supported by the NTCA. NRTC is owned by approximately 425 rural utility cooperatives. The primary focus of NRTC is satellite communication for rural video and data applications.

(NRTC is located at P.O. Box 9994, Washington, DC 20016, telephone (202) 944-2539. Bob Phillips is Chief Executive Officer.)

NTCA

The National Telephone Cooperative Association (NTCA) is the voice of 450 small and rural telephone carriers, about half of them cooperative and half commercial companies. NTCA has been actively defending rural telephone interests at the FCC, in recent court proceedings and before Congress. NTCA has been particularly concerned with issues of financing for rural telephone carriers and has been a strong defender of the telephone loan programs of the REA in the Department of Agriculture. In addition to its work on Capitol Hill and at the FCC, NTCA provides a full range of services to its members, including seminars, a variety of publications, and a comprehensive package of insurance and benefits plans. NTCA, with 55 employees, has the largest staff dedicated to serving the rural telephone industry.

(NTCA is located at 2626 Pennsylvania Avenue N.W., Washington DC 20037, telephone (202) 298-2300. Michael E. Brunner is the Executive Vice President. Shirley A. Bloomfield is the Assistant Director of Government Affairs.)

OPASTCO

The Organization for the Protection and Advancement of Small Telephone Companies (OPASTCO), founded in 1963, has approximately 375 members, all local exchange carriers with fewer than 50,000 access lines. In addition to representing its members' interests in matters before the FCC, Congress, the REA, and other government and industry forums, OPASTCO has strong education and publications programs which provide its members with timely industry information with a specific small company focus.

(OPASTCO is located at 2000 K Street N.W., Suite 205, Washington DC 20006, telephone (202) 659-5990. John N. Rose is Executive Vice President.)

USTA

The major telephone carrier industry association is the United States Telephone Association (USTA), founded in 1897 as the "independent" (that is, non-Bell) telephone company association. Since the local Bell companies were spun off from AT&T in 1984, they too have been members of the enlarged USTA, which now has more than 1,100 members representing more than 99 percent of the telephone access lines in the country. USTA has a "Small Company Committee" and a small company affairs department with supporting staff to assist its smaller members.

(USTA is located at 900 19th Street, N.W., Suite 800, Washington, DC 20006, telephone (202) 835-3100. John Sodolski is President. Chief staff members concerned with small company affairs are Robbert Nachtweh and Henry I. Buchanan.)

State Associations
In addition to the national associations cited above, there are a number of state associations of local exchange carriers. These state associations are primarily concerned with issues arising from their members' common interests before state regulatory bodies.

3. Financing Sources

The telephone business is capital intensive with two major categories of costs, the original cost of the physical plant and equipment, including telephone lines and switches, and recurring operating expenses. The annual revenues local exchange carriers receive from their subscribers and long-distance users, in theory, cover all of the operating expenses of the carriers, a depreciation charge (for example, for equipment with an estimated 20-year life, one twentieth of the capital cost), plus a return on the original capital investment to cover interest expenses and equity capital costs. The financing problem for rural carriers is where to obtain the capital funds needed to install and upgrade the telephone lines and switches necessary to provide service. Even though over time the portion of user revenues allocated to depreciation should be sufficient to recover all the original capital costs, the carriers need capital funds (either equity capital or loans) up front for the original equipment purchase.

REA

A major source of capital funds for rural telephone carriers is the Rural Electrification Administration (REA), established as part of the U.S. Department of Agriculture in the 1940s to provide loans and technical assistance to rural utilities, both electric and telephone. In 1988 Congress gave REA authority for approximately $536 million of loans or loan guarantees. Some of the loans are provided at five percent interest, with the government contribution being the subsidized interest rate. Others are provided at the REA cost of funds rate or by guarantees of commercial loans. REA borrowers are proud that in the long history of the program there has never been a default. The telephone carriers have always been able to repay the loans from revenues generated by subscribers using the telephone facilities purchased with the borrowed money. The associations representing REA borrowers claim that most REA borrowers could not afford to pay commercial interest rates. REA data indicate that REA borrowers have an average ratio of net worth to total assets of 30 percent, far below the 50 to 60 percent usually required by commercial lending institutions.

The financing available through REA comes in various forms. In 1988, $239,250,000 was appropriated for insured loans through the REA revolving loan fund at the five percent interest rate. An additional $177,045,000 was available from the Rural Telephone Bank (RTB) at rates based on the RTB cost of funds. Staffing for RTB is provided by REA. A further $119,625,000 of commercial loan guarantees was available through the Federal Financing Bank (FFB), based on REA recommendations.

RTFC

The Rural Telephone Finance Cooperative (RTFC) is an affiliate of the National Rural Utilities Cooperative Financing Corporation (usually abbreviated as CFC). CFC was formed in 1969 by a group of rural electric cooperatives, based on recommendations of an NRECA committee, to provide private financing for rural electric cooperatives.

The telephone affiliate, RTFC, began its lending in 1987. It is a supplemental lender to carriers whose primary source of capital funds is REA. RTFC has two sources of financing. One is through the purchase of capital certificates by rural carriers, which must purchase at least an amount equal to five percent of any funds borrowed from RTFC. The other is bonds sold in the private bond market. The bonds are sold at market rates, and are apparently more attractive to lenders than debt instruments of individual rural carriers because they are collectively backed by the participating rural carriers as a group, and because they are secondary lenders to entities that have qualified for and are also receiving funds from the REA.

The RTFC funds are loaned to rural carriers at market rates and are usually used for telephone system upgrades that do not meet the narrow eligibility criteria currently being applied by REA. One example is upgrades to connect rural switches to competitive long-distance carriers, a purpose currently not accepted by REA as within their criteria. From inception to date RTFC has loaned a total of approximately $250 million.

(RTFC is located at 1115 30th St. N.W., Washington, DC 20007, telephone (202) 337-6700. Charles B. Gill is Chief Executive Officer.)

CoBank

CoBank, the National Bank for Cooperatives, was established on January 1, 1989, when the Central Bank for Cooperatives merged with ten district Banks for Cooperatives in various parts of the country. CoBank is part of the Farm Credit System established by the U.S. Department of Agriculture. CoBank's predecessors have been serving some of the credit needs of rural America for more than 50 years and have been authorized to make loans to many eligible rural utility systems for more than 15 years. A recent federal legislative change now permits all of the rural telephone systems that have been certified as eligible for REA financing to also borrow from the National Bank for Cooperatives. CoBank is thus an additional potential source of supplemental financing for REA telephone borrowers.

(CoBank, the National Bank for Cooperatives, is located at P.O. Box 5110, Denver, CO 80217, telephone (303) 740-4000. Jack Cassidy is Vice President, Corporate Relations.)

4. Regulatory Environment

FCC

Rural telephone carriers, like all other telephone carriers, are regulated by the Federal Communications Commission (FCC), which has jurisdiction over interstate communications. FCC policies encouraging competition, especially in long distance telephony and business telecommunications, are requiring rural carriers to adapt to a new environment. A number of the FCC actions affecting rural carriers are discussed in Chapter Four.

PUCs

Intrastate telephone rates are regulated by state Public Utility Commissions (PUCs). In some states regulations are similar to those of the FCC for the interstate portion. In others, the PUC regulations may be quite different. A key issue is the treatment of depreciation costs. In 1983 the FCC issued an order preempting states on depreciation methods. Some state PUCs objected, and the order was overturned by the U.S. Supreme Court in 1986. NARUC, the National Association of Regulatory Utility Commissioners, is the organization used by PUCs to share information with other states and to pursue common interests, such as relations between PUCs and the FCC.

(NARUC is located at 1102 ICC Building, 12th and Constitution, N.W., Washington, DC 20044, telephone (202) 898-2200. Paul Rodgers is the Administrator.)

Joint Board

Since rates are regulated on a cost-plus basis in both federal and most state jurisdictions, one recurring issue is how to allocate joint costs between the two jurisdictions. These issues are usually resolved by a federal-state joint board (comprised of four state and three FCC commissioners).

Federal Court

The AT&T consent decree (Modified Final Judgment) breaking up the former Bell system into AT&T and seven RBOCs has created another regulatory jurisdiction to which both Bell companies and independent rural telephone carriers must pay attention. Continuing oversight of the consent decree is provided by Federal Judge Harold Greene, who has substantial control over what activities the RBOCs are permitted to engage in. One concern of the rural carriers is that the BOCs may be permitted to provide long-distance service under individual ("de-averaged") pricing schedules. Such a policy change could increase the prices for rural long-distance calls and could reduce the share of revenues rural telephone carriers receive from those calls. It could also increase pressure on AT&T to propose rates based on the costs of each long-distance route rather than national average costs. Such "de-averaged" long-distance rates could result in substantially higher rural long-distance rates. Another concern of the rural carriers is that if RBOCs are permitted to engage in manufacturing, the source of equipment supply for smaller carriers will become more limited and more costly.

5. Federal Policy Makers

Executive Branch

In addition to the various regulatory authorities, three federal government departments have substantial policy responsibility for rural telecommunications. One is the Department of Agriculture, whose REA is not only the major source of financial assistance for rural telephone carriers, but is also the source of technical advice to rural carriers on standards and equipment. Another is the Department of Justice, which has the responsibility to recommend policy to Judge Greene in connection with both periodic reviews and requests for waivers of the AT&T consent decree. The third is the Department of Commerce, whose National Telecommunications and Information Administration (NTIA) has overall federal telecommunications policy responsibility. The recent NTIA report, Telecom 2000, recommends a goal of "universal information service" by the year 2000, and recognizes that special policy actions will be required to ensure that telecommunications and information services are available to rural America.

Legislative Branch

In both the Senate and the House of Representatives the key committee concerned with rural development in general and the REA in particular is the Agriculture Committee. The House Agriculture Committee is chaired by Representative E. de la Garza (Texas). The subcommittee with oversight over REA is the Conservation, Credit and Rural Development Subcommittee, chaired by Representative Glenn English of Oklahoma. The Senate Agriculture Committee is chaired by Senator Patrick Leahy of Vermont. The subcommittee with oversight over the REA is the Rural Development and Rural Electrification Subcommittee, chaired by Senator Howell Heflin of Alabama.

In both the House and the Senate, the appropriations committees, and in particular the agriculture subcommittees, which together set the REA loan level appropriations for each fiscal year, are critical players. The Senate Agriculture Appropriations Subcommittee is chaired by Senator Quentin Burdick (North Dakota). The House Appropriations Subcommittee is chaired by Representative Jamie Whitten (Mississippi). In both houses the Commerce, Justice and State subcommittee of the Appropriations Committee sets the FCC funding levels for operation for each fiscal year. The Senate Subcommittee is chaired by Senator Ernest Hollings (South Carolina) and the House Subcommittee is chaired by Representative Neal Smith (Iowa).

In both houses the Budget Committees set the policy and ceiling spending levels allocated to individual appropriations subcommittees. The Senate Budget Committee is chaired by Senator James Sasser (Tennessee) and the House Budget Committee is chaired by Representative Leon Panetta (California).

The Senate Commerce Committee, chaired by Senator Hollings, its Telecommunications Subcommittee, chaired by Senator Daniel Inouye (Hawaii), and the Telecommunications Subcommittee of the House Energy and Commerce Committee, chaired by Representative Edward Markey (Massachusetts), are the authorizing and overview committees for telecommunications policy.

The Senate Finance Committee, chaired by Senator Lloyd Bentsen (Texas), and House Ways and Means Committee, chaired by Representative Daniel Rostenkowski (Illinois), handle revenue matters that impact the tax exempt status of cooperatives, telephone excise taxes and other small business concerns.

The Judiciary Committees, chaired by Senator Joseph Biden (Delaware) in the Senate and Representative Jack Brooks (Texas) in the House, have oversight of the Justice Department and will be influential in upcoming MFJ (Modified Final Judgment) legislative proceedings concerned with the oversight of the AT&T consent decree.

In the House of Representatives, the Information, Justice and Agriculture subcommittee of the Government Operations Committee (chaired by Representative Robert Wise of West Virginia) has investigative oversight of REA telephone programs.

6. Other Players

Suppliers of equipment to rural telephone carriers have an obvious stake in the outcome of rural telephone policy. The major upgrade required in the next decade is in digital switches. The two suppliers with the largest sales to rural carriers are Northern Telecom and Stromberg Carlson.

The long-distance carriers which connect with and share revenues with rural carriers also have a stake in the outcome of rural telephone policy. At present, AT&T is the only long-distance carrier for most rural subscribers because few rural telephone exchanges have been upgraded to accommodate equal access to competitive long-distance carriers. Even if the exchanges were upgraded, it is unclear whether MCI, U.S. Sprint and other competitive long-distance providers would pay for the costs of extending their long-distance facilities to connect with those rural exchanges.

METHODOLOGIES AND STATISTICAL ELABORATIONS ON CHAPTER FIVE

Rural Access to Telephone Service in America Today

To estimate the number of households that do not have access to telephone service, EMCI relied on a five-level analysis, as shown in Figure 15. First, recent data on the number of households without telephone service was obtained and disaggregated to the county level. The data were then adjusted for local economic conditions.

EMCI used the econometric models mentioned in Chapter Five, in which the number of households without telephone service are estimated based on the percentage of households living in poverty. The poverty thresholds were based on 1987 data from the Bureau of Census, shown in Table 12.

The difference between the predicted number of households without service and the actual number is the number of households that do not have service due to non-economic factors. This residual difference is then input to the next level of analysis.

Table 12 1987 Poverty Thresholds	
Family Size	Income
1	$ 5,778
2	7,397
3	9,056
4	11,611
5	13,737
6	15,509
7	17,649
8	19,515
9+	23,105

Figure 15 Methodology to Estimate Remote Households Without Telephone Service

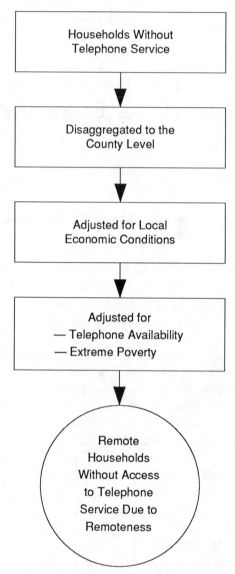

Source: EMCI, Inc. from *The Market for BETR/Cellular/Fixed Rural Radio Telephone Service.*

The residual difference is adjusted by a number of factors. The first involves the distinction between not having a telephone and not being reachable by telephone. In surveys, the Census asks households if they have a telephone. If the answer is no, they are asked if they are reachable by telephone. This distinction is important in college dormitories and boarding houses, for example, where there may be telephone access, although there may not be telephones in individual dwelling units. There is substantial variation between these two cases across states.

In addition to adjusting for telephone availability, EMCI adjusted for levels of extreme poverty. The degree of confidence in the econometric models described above declines as the level of poverty increases, especially for counties where the percent of the population living below the poverty level exceeds 30 percent. These economic models consistently underestimated the number of households without telephone service in areas with a high percentage of households living in poverty. For this reason, in those rural counties where extreme poverty exists, EMCI generally assumed that all households without telephone service do not have service due to poverty. In some areas where extreme poverty is accompanied by a low population density (for example, on Indian reservations in the West), the estimate was not adjusted. These "extreme" poverty adjustments reduced the estimate of households without access to telephone service by less than 10 percent.

Finally, EMCI assumed that in metropolitan areas, all of the households without telephone service do not have service for reasons other than geographic isolation. While there may be isolated households within some metropolitan areas, this assumption is generally reasonable.

THE IMPORTANCE OF COMMUNICATIONS AND INFORMATION SYSTEMS TO RURAL DEVELOPMENT IN THE UNITED STATES

Report of an Aspen Institute Conference
Aspen, Colorado
July 24-27, 1988

By David Bollier
Contributing Editor, *CHANNELS* Magazine

I remember the Norman Rockwell painting of the young Henry Ford with a model of a horseless carriage in his hand, showing it to the village blacksmith. Ford is totally preoccupied. The blacksmith has this worried, puzzled, uncomprehending look on his face, but he knows damn well what its implications are—that there won't be many blacksmiths when this technology is fully implemented.

The applications of telecommunications and information technologies are so pervasive and so versatile that we don't know what the limits are, or what the full implications are. You can't show computers to anyone without provoking some kind of fear—but also anticipation.

What's significant to me is that these technologies alter all human relationships—and not just those that are defined by

123

the marketplace. And therefore the marketplace is not adequate for anticipating and understanding the consequences of these technologies. That, to me, is what compels public policy.

Marty Strange
Center for Rural Affairs
Walthill, Nebraska

The Importance of Communications and Information Systems to Rural Development in the United States

In late July 1988, The Aspen Institute's Program on Communications and Society hosted a three-day conference on the role that telecommunications and information technologies might play in fostering rural economic development.

It is an issue of growing importance as more rural economies falter, often victimized by larger forces transforming the U.S. and international economies. Rural economies have been especially hurt by the decline of the U.S. dollar and intensified international competition, both of which have undermined the traditional rural industries of agriculture, mining and manufacturing.

The conference, funded by a grant from the Ford Foundation and organized in consultation with The Aspen Institute's Rural Economic Policy Program, looked prospectively at the rural economies of the 1990s and beyond. It asked how rural America will be affected—positively and negatively—as more of the U.S. economy comes to depend on such technologies as teleconferencing, facsimile transmission, digital data transmission, electronic mail, and related systems.

Will current trends result in a yawning telecommunications "infrastructure gap" between rural and urban America? Will that gap prevent rural America from becoming an integrated part of the national economy, resulting in chronic economic privation? Or will telecommunications and information technologies provide a rare opportunity for "importing" new industries into rural America, weaving its economy and people more tightly into the national fabric?

The conference sought to approach these larger questions by asking, first, more specific, refined questions. What particular needs and opportunities do the new electronic technologies provide rural America? What factors—technological, economic, social and otherwise—will promote or impede their actual use? If we can understand these issues, what affirmative steps can we then take to invigorate rural economies by way of telecommunications and information systems?

The Aspen Institute invited 25 participants from various fields of expertise to address these issues. The interdisciplinary sharing of knowledge drew upon rural development economists, social scientists, state and county development officials, rural policy analysts, private business consultants, telephone company officials, and business users of telecommunications and information systems. These diverse experts are based at universities and other research institutions, or hold leadership positions in government, industry, foundations and rural advocacy groups.

Michael Rice, Director of the Aspen Institute's Program on Communications and Society and moderator of the conference, expressed his hope that the discussions would:

- Bring together the expertise of rural development scholars and telecommunications experts, and provoke fresh insights and ideas;
- Develop working hypotheses for the "leverage effect"— i.e., how can new investments in telecommunications and information systems help a rural economy and its people?
- Identify specific topics for future research and explore what supportive roles federal, state and local governments can play.

1. Rural Policy and Economic Development

Why Care About Rural Development?

In an attempt to identify first principles, Michael Rice opened the first session by asking a painfully basic question: "Why should we care about the development prospects of rural America?"

The answers seemed to fall into several general categories of concern: maintaining diverse cultures and community autonomy, serving economic needs, promoting social equity, and enhancing environmental protection.

Dr. Philip Burgess, Executive Director of US West, one of the regional Bell operating companies, noted that "rural areas are the locations for some very rich cultures which enliven and enrich this nation." In the West, for example, Hispanics and Native Americans add a great deal to American culture.

Many rural residents, especially Native Americans, are deeply committed to their regions by way of their histories, kinship and culture, said Professor Heather Hudson, Director of the Telecommunications Management and Policy Program at the McLaren College of Business at the University of San Francisco. For these people, who want to remain independent, yet are frustrated by their economic problems, rural development is a very important concern.

Michael Clark, President of the Environmental Policy Institute in Washington, D.C., warned, "It is a dangerous concept to see rural areas marginalized and therefore made ripe for exploitation." As cautionary examples, Clark cited the history of mining in Appalachia and the current dumping of urban industrial wastes in rural areas.

There are strong economic reasons for bolstering rural regions, said Mary Mountcastle, Vice President for Economic Development of MDC, a nonprofit economic development organization in Chapel Hill, North Carolina. "The nation can't afford to waste its human resources in an age of increasing competitiveness and declining supply of human capital." Rural development is important because cities don't have the social infrastructure to deal with untrained new workers.

Like many participants, Dr. Ted Bradshaw, Research Sociologist at the University of California, Berkeley, cited the economic hardships of rural America as a compelling reason for new development initiatives. He mentioned the overall decline of rural export commodities, the slack lumber business in the Pacific Northwest, and the effects on the South of stiff international competition in manufacturing.

Why do European nations care about rural development? John Bryden, Program Director of the Arkleton Trust, a rural policy research group based in Inverness, Scotland, noted three general reasons: 1) Respect for basic human rights, such as equal economic opportunity; 2) A desire to make better use of human resources which, because of distance and lack of mobility, are underutilized; and 3) A desire to maintain native rural cultures and lifestyles.

"I think there is value in fostering cultural heterogeneity [in rural regions] as we move into a global economy," said Dr. Don Dillman, Director of the Social and Economic Sciences Research Center at Washington State University.

Dillman added, "I worry about a split society, in which educated people marry educated people and live in urban areas, because that's the only place they can get jobs, and uneducated people marry each other and live in rural areas."

Public policy is by definition intended to rectify economic and social injustice, said Marty Strange, Senior Associate for the Center for Rural Affairs, an advocacy group based in Walthill, Nebraska. Public policy exists because "the old world of Adam Smith isn't enough. There's more to life than improving efficiency."

Kenneth Deavers, Director of the USDA Economics Research Service's Agriculture and Rural Economy Division, agreed that at the federal level, economic equity is the most influential argument for rural development policy. "It is a reason that [rural policy] has broad-based support. It provides a way to engage those who believe market forces only should prevail."

The answer to "why care about rural policy" is almost too obvious, said Andrew Roscoe, Senior Consultant for EMCI, a management consulting firm based in Arlington, Virginia. "We are a unified country and that's why we try to help each other. There is an inefficiency inherent in development strategies, because the natural economic forces tend to make things more efficient if we don't interfere with them.

"That's not to say we don't interfere," he added. "The question is, How much cost and loss of efficiency are we willing to incur to target development [to rural areas]? How much do we want to let natural economic forces play themselves out?"

Rural Values and Economic Development

Rural economic development is not just about the merits of *laissez-faire* versus public policy intervention, participants soon made clear. It is also about the terms under which any economic development proceeds. It is about the values that are reflected in public policy.

The group quickly expressed concern about how economic development affects the indigenous values of rural communities. On balance, is development beneficial or destructive?

Scott Howard, Director of Catalog Operations for L.L. Bean, the retailer, questioned whether "we should be imposing metropolitan socioeconomic values on rural parts of the country." He pointed out that while some parts of Maine might be considered impoverished by objective standards, rural residents value, and want to protect, their way of life and independence.

Richard Silkman, Director of the State Planning Office in Maine, elaborated on this point: "Development in rural areas is a much more difficult and expensive proposition because the infrastructure simply isn't there." Rapid development triggers overnight problems with solid waste disposal, groundwater contamination, traffic congestion, crowded schools and other problems that suburban communities have taken decades to address.

The claim that these emerging needs can be painlessly financed by the fruits of economic growth just isn't true, said Silkman, because rural people end up paying higher property taxes and suffer from cultural dislocations and environmental pollution. That is why many rural communities are very skeptical of metropolitan models of development.

Indeed, economic growth does not necessarily eradicate poverty, said Stuart Rosenfeld, Deputy Director of the Southern Growth Policies Board, a "think tank" that creates strategies for economic growth for 12 southern states and Puerto Rico. Of the 38 fastest-growing counties in the South, nine of them are what USDA classifies as persistent poverty counties; 12 of those 38 had per capita incomes of less than $7,000 a year.

Yet a staunch antidevelopment stance is not necessarily the solution either, said Cynthia Duncan, Associate Director of the Aspen Institute's Rural Economic Policy Program. Although development does bring problems, it also serves—or tries to serve—acute human needs. In Maine, for example, "there are kids trapped in rural areas who need jobs."

Duncan's comment points up a conundrum: Rural areas need help, especially from urban businesses and the federal government, yet they also prize their independence and want to protect it.

Community autonomy is why there are some 1,100 separate school districts in Texas, said Dr. Frederick Williams, Professor at the University of Texas at Austin's College of Communications. "It is inefficient, but the districts want to retain their separate identities and not consolidate. It gives them a sense of power and self-control."

The Current Plight of Rural America

While small rural towns may like to see themselves as distinctive (and indeed, they may be), the USDA's Ken Deaver warned that their economies must be viewed in the context of the national economy. Many rural economies are suffering because they are out of sync with the national economy.

Approximately 40 percent of rural counties remain heavily dependent on agriculture or mining, two declining industries. The economies of another 30 percent of rural counties are based on manufacturing, which tends to be low-wage, low-skill, mass production activity that is especially vulnerable to international competition and cyclical downturns.

As the national economy grows increasingly dependent on services, the rate of new firm creation in rural areas is very low, and the urban-rural differential is growing, Deavers said. Rural areas seem plagued by fewer enterpreneurs, fewer opportunities, more difficulty in finding out about opportunities, higher information costs, and the siphoning away of rural money to regional and urban businesses.

Because it is very unlikely that ailing rural industries will generate many new jobs in the future, rural communities hoping to remain viable must develop some new "opportunity structures," Deavers observed. The problem is how to get there from here. "How can [rural towns] participate in service economy growth, particularly the export of (business) services beyond the local community?"

Historically, rural communities have been "able to survive because of 'location-specific rents,'" said Richard Silkman of the Maine State Planning Office. "What's happened over the past 20 years is that technology, the finding of other mineral deposits, the growth of foreign agriculture, and other factors have made location-specific rents in the U.S. much less valuable."

This is ominous for rural America, said Silkman, because "telecommunication is going to diminish further the value of location-specific rents and make location a nonfactor [in economic decisionmaking]. If this is so, what is going to be the economic base of rural America?"

One residual advantage that rural communities retain, noted Ted Bradshaw of UC Berkeley, is their lifestyle amenities. "With the rise of more 'mobile occupations,' and even mobile industries, more people will be attracted by rural isolation. Retirees have already done this, bringing their Social Security checks with them."

"But this creates tension," replied Silkman, because a set of monied newcomers competes with the native population over different visions of quality of life. So you have to come back to the basic question, "How do you manage growth to preserve quality of life?"

One new basis of location-specific rents for rural communities could be human resources, said Jim Roche, Marketing Director of the Northspan Group of Duluth, Minnesota. "In northeastern Minnesota, an available, educated workforce is a major incentive to attract businesses," Roche said.

Before rural America can revive itself, it must first acknowledge that a problem exists, said Rod Bates, Managing General Partner of Bates Video Production in Lincoln, Nebraska, and former Director of Economic Development for Nebraska.

Many small towns are going through a sequence of psychological responses to economic decline, he said—from denial to anger to bargaining to acceptance, in the formulation of Elizabeth Kubler-Ross (*On Death and Dying*). After so many years of economic tumult, said Bates, "the environment is ripe in many towns for seeking change and redefinition."

But the situation is not uniformly bleak, even in declining industries, said Philip Burgess of US West. While mining has lost 321,000 jobs since 1980, there has been an increase of nearly 5,000 jobs among mining companies with fewer than 100 employees.

Burgess' conclusions: The small entrepreneurial firms, not the "old, big dinosaurs," are creating new jobs. Yet the large companies have the political clout to win preferential government policies—and that's a problem.

It is one reason that rural policy is such a shambles, said several participants: most rural political leaders do not fight to improve the lot of nonagricultural constituencies.

Rural Policy in a Shambles

"My sense, living in the Northeast, is that we don't really have a rural policy," said Richard Silkman. "We have an agricultural policy. Our rural policy, such as it is, seems to be, 'Let people migrate to where the jobs might be.'"

Other participants agreed that agricultural needs are too often perceived, incorrectly, to be the sum total of rural needs. Jack Briggs, Executive Director of the Macon (Missouri) County Economic Development Office, noted that according to the 1980 census, only 900 of his county's 16,000 residents were based on farms, and half of the latter held off-farm jobs.

"So in our area, if you talk about rural policy, you're talking about 450 people out of 16,000. All our legislators want to be on the agriculture committee. We say, 'Why?'"

"The reason we do have an agricultural policy and not a rural policy is because it's urban people who are making policy, and urban people have to eat," said Dr. Edwin Parker, a consultant now based in Gleneden Beach, Oregon, former communications professor and president of an earth station manufacturing concern.

But Michael Clark, the environmentalist, added that a deficient rural policy is not solely the fault of urban members of

Congress, who "don't know or care about or understand agricultural policy." Rural areas themselves elect legislators whose chief concern is agriculture—and that interest shortchanges other rural constituencies who could benefit from broader, more innovative rural initiatives.

If the failures of current rural policy can be blamed on current configurations of political power—among both urban and rural policymakers—participants agreed that a deeply rooted intellectual tradition must also be challenged: the imposition of urban policy models on rural areas.

Federal demographers refer to rural areas as "nonmetro" counties, a negative comparison which always seems to make rural areas seem worse, complained Michael Clark. He urged instead, "Let's look at healthy rural communities as models; income levels and other national standards may not be the best criteria to judge rural towns."

The Importance of Rural Self-Determination

This is the missing dimension in so much rural policy, said one participant after another: the actual desires of each particular rural community.

"If you start with the idea the local communities like being where they are, the proper policy will follow," said Rod Bates, the video producer from Lincoln, Nebraska. "I don't know if you can have an enlightened federal rural policy. People in rural communities have to define why they like it there. Then they can decide whether to bring in a new plant or fiber optics."

Public policy works much better, said Mary Mountcastle of MDC, when people have a certain "ownership" stake in it. In choosing what kinds of telecommunications investments should be made, community leadership must cultivate broad-based support.

Federal and state policies can be crafted to offer resources and technical assistance to local communities without imposing on them, said Stuart Rosenfeld of the Southern Growth Policies Board. He offered as an example the Appalachian Regional Commission's role in building 700 vocational training centers.

"What strikes me," said Philip Burgess of US West, "is the tremendous variety and diversity in rural America. The lesson of that is that no single federal policy is going to work." Burgess urged that any innovations in rural policy focus on the "institutional policy architecture" rather than policy per se, because the power politics of rural policy determine whether it will be successful or not.

In the 1960s, Burgess continued, we were moving toward area-based development programs such as the Model Cities program. "Despite its flaws, this approach must be resurrected because it provides a political basis for politicians to favor one region over another. It provides a way to decentralize the forums in which political negotiations take place."

"Without such hybrid forums," warned Burgess, "we'll just have another wasteful Economic Development Administration (EDA) or Appalachian Regional Commission (ARC)." He urged that we study why these agencies failed, and learn some lessons about how federal leadership interacts—inefficiently and corruptly—with local civic leadership.

Susan Sechler of The Aspen Institute agreed that in many 1960s programs the local political process was "deeply flawed in determining priorities and seeing who got benefits"—a flaw that, to some extent, the Office of Economic Opportunity surmounted.

The real challenge, said Sechler, is to find a way to enhance political participation in rural economic development without creating another layer of policymaking that will be unresponsive to what local citizens want and need.

Given the diversity of rural America, Michael Rice asked whether any uniform national rural policy is really possible.

Ken Deavers responded that a rural policy which simply aggregates the diverse choices of hundreds of rural communities would be far too costly and impractical. "A bottoms-up approach with no sense of the national economy and its opportunities is hopeless. If you start with what every rural community wants to be, regardless of the constraints, and add it all together, the cost of achieving it would amount to five times the GNP! You will waste enormous resources trying to get people to be something they can't be."

Marty Strange of the Center for Rural Affairs suggested that one uniform goal of federal rural policy could be the "empowerment of people to make their own development decisions."

Federal policy must take cognizance of the "power structure" by which policy is made; otherwise rural policy will simply end up gentrifying rural communities and fail to address persistent rural needs. Strange concluded that "any discussion of technology policy and development must talk about who wins, who loses, and who's in charge."

Michael Clark agreed. A key question, he said, is "Who makes decisions about rural development? As our society becomes more complex and technological, most of these decisions are made by a small elite—leaders in industry and government, and heavy users of telecommunications."

Burgess argued that these elite groups—civic leaders, business leaders, economic development consultants, and foundations—are often more a part of the problem than a part of the solution. "They don't really know what they are doing."

"There is no profession of economic development," he said. "We don't have a body of knowledge that can be passed on and refined, and to which people can be held accountable. These leaders are influencing people to take action, to spend public money—often hurting rural communities."

Can New Leadership Emerge?

There seems to be a quandary here, said Michael Rice. "If rural policy does not have legitimacy without maximum citizen participation, yet today's political officials do not have the 'right' views about wise economic development, how then are the 'right' choices going to emerge? Where will leadership come from?"

Heather Hudson suggested that telecommunications can help give people access to government proceedings—and this can help develop leadership. In Alaska, for example, telecommunications allows citizens from distant communities to participate in hearings at the state capital.

Fred Williams said that in Los Angeles, an experiment was held to let citizens participate in civic hearings via broadband communications. "The problem wasn't channels of communications but lack of interest." From his experiences in Missouri, Jack Briggs agreed—the idea of "informed, active local participation" is a myth.

Hudson replied that telecommunications can facilitate participation; it does not guarantee participation. What's important is that you go "looking for thirsty horses"—people with leadership potential who will be receptive to help.

Developing leadership to foster better rural telecommunications is not a partisan issue, said Scott Howard of L.L. Bean. It is a prerequisite for rural economic development. One of the biggest challenges, said Don Dillman, "is to convince ingrown locals that new and different strategies should be tried."

One fertile source of leadership is rural entrepreneurs who left rural towns and then returned many years later, bringing back new cultural and educated perspectives. Dillman said that some companies such as Bausch & Lomb have tried to identify such people by acquiring subscription lists to local newspapers and then wooing out-of-town subscribers to come back.

The problem of attracting educated people back to rural areas points up another persistent challenge, said Dillman. "Why do people like living in rural areas? Residential preference in rural areas is a greatly underresearched issue."

Participants suggested some anecdotal answers to why rural residents live where they do. Rural residents may have extended families and strong community ties; they may be close to nearby job opportunities; and other opportunities elsewhere may be perceived to be too low-paying or unstable to justify moving.

Residential preference is a key factor often overlooked in rural development schemes, said Ken Deavers, citing a recent proposal by Senator Max Baucus of Montana. Baucus proposed a survey of firms to find out what facilities they want in rural communities; then the federal government would help underwrite the building of such facilities.

"If you want to develop rural Montana," said Deavers, "one of the first things you need to do is find out what kind of people want to live in rural Montana. Then you start thinking about the infrastructure investments and public policies that will serve those kinds of people."

It just doesn't work to ask business about amenities it wants in rural areas, when it can just as easily pursue the same amenities elsewhere, said Deavers. A case in point: many industrial parks around the country financed by the Economic Development Administration which have no tenants.

2. The Promise of Telecommunications for Rural America

A Snapshot of Existing Rural Telephone Service

There are three basic functions that better telecommunications can provide to rural communities, said Andrew Jacobson, Associate Publisher of Telecom Publishing Group, which publishes several telephone-related trade newsletters.

The first, arguably most important, function is to extend basic telephone service to remote locations and to poor people. A second function is to provide new operating efficiencies for businesses. And a third function is to provide residents of remote rural areas access to new educational opportunities.

Extending the telecommunications revolution to rural areas should be governed by six tiers of priority, said Don Dillman. Listed in order of importance, the priorities should be to:

1)   Extend basic telephone service to everyone;
2)   Move from party-line service to dedicated service;
3)   Improve the quality of telephone lines so that data transmission is possible;
4)   Lower long-distance rates so that basic voice communication to the nearest areas is more affordable;
5)   Provide local-access rates to computer data banks, so that "connect time" fees are more affordable; and
6)   Expand the capacity of telephone lines so that faster and larger data transmissions are possible.

Current deficiencies in rural telephone service can limit personal communications and a community's economic development. For example, poor-quality lines may make data transmission impossible; limited trunk-line capacity may prevent volume data transmissions; lack of touch-tone service can prevent interactive communications; and analog switching equipment may keep long-distance rates higher than what could be achieved through digital switching equipment.

At present, five percent of U.S. households do not have telephones, primarily because they cannot afford one, according to Andrew Roscoe of EMCI. The number of households without phone service because of their remoteness is 173,000, he said, although the Rural Electrification Administration's estimate is 500,000.

How many party lines still remain? There are 1.7 million party lines out of the Bell companies' 97 million households, and 1.8 million party lines out of the 25 million households served by independent phone companies.

Rural residents spend three to four times more for telephone service than city dwellers, said Heather Hudson. This is partly because rural phone service is governed by a different rate structure, but also because rural residents spend a larger percentage of their (lower) income on phone service.

John Bryden of the Arkleton Trust offered a compelling critique explaining why telecommunications and information technologies are of growing importance to rural communities.

Services are the fastest-growing sector of industrial economies and are becoming integrated into all forms of final production, noted Bryden. This has profound consequences for a company's or region's competitiveness, because the production of traded goods and services increasingly depends on the efficiency and quality of such services as accounting, banking, legal services, printing, and design.

This trend can both help and hurt rural communities. On the one hand, it makes them more vulnerable to competition from "outside" firms, because new communications technologies are overcoming distance-related costs. But by the same token, the new technologies give rural services new opportunities to grow far beyond local markets.

The question is, will rural towns exploit, or be exploited by, these technologies? At present, the latter is occurring, and rural

America is in danger of becoming a net importer of services. That is why it is imperative that rural communities learn how to identify and efficiently serve "export" markets.

But first they must develop a better telecommunications infrastructure (digital switching, better lines, dedicated phones, etc.). This also means having to educate and train rural leaders and the public about the need for better telecommunications.

Rural Business and Telecommunications

What are some of the specific ways that advanced telecommunications can help rural economies? Most cases mentioned by participants were variations on a theme—that rural America cannot keep pace with the rest of the U.S. economy unless it acquires new electronic technologies, particularly digital switching.

Consider the hospital supply business. Richard Silkman said that a major management task faced by all hospitals is the maintenance of their inventories of medical supplies. Using sophisticated telecommunications, a midwest hospital supply company negotiated an exclusive contract with Chicago hospitals to maintain an online inventory control system for hospitals. Result: nearly instant replenishment of supplies.

If you happen to be a Kentucky beaker supplier, however, you are forever excluded from the Chicago hospital market unless you can offer the same online capability. Even if you sell via the wholesale vendor, you would still need the online capability. The lesson: rural-based businesses that want to maintain their traditional supply relationships will have to keep up with new telecommunications developments.

Why is this a public policy problem? asked Andrew Jacobson. He said private consultants can help rural businesses set up perfectly serviceable satellite linkages.

"But small businesses don't have telecommunications managers," replied Richard Adler of the Institute for the Future. In a survey he conducted in Palo Alto, small businesses such as branch banks, wholesale meatpackers and medium-sized law firms simply do not know what telecommunications options could improve their businesses—or how to acquire them. The problem is presumably more acute in rural areas, said Adler.

If ignorance is not the problem in rural areas, the simple lack of enhanced telecommunications often is. Fred Williams of the University of Texas at Austin told of a national chain of hardware stores which is beginning to require its franchisees to obtain an online ordering system as a condition for retaining their dealerships. Eventually the franchisees must be able to communicate with the national headquarters, with a modem at 2400 baud, on the public telephone network.

Before this can happen, however, local independent phone companies must upgrade the quality of their lines so that modem transmissions can work; this in turn will require approval by the public utility commission. (The request is being studied.) Many Texas school districts, Williams added, are also starting to require their schools to develop an online capability.

The story was told, also, of a Montana businesswoman who may be forced to move her thriving rural business to a larger town, perhaps out of state, because of poor telecommunications. The phone lines do not allow fax transmissions, and overnight mail to her location is not reliable enough.

These examples suggest how better telecommunications are becoming more vital in everyday business transactions, even for small businesses.

While rural businesses struggle to keep up, major corporations are using enhanced telecommunications to relocate and decentralize, so they can take advantage of relative economic advantages (cheaper labor, supply routes, etc.). While this may provide new investment to needy rural economies, it also makes them more acutely dependent on outsiders.

An example of this trend, said Stuart Rosenfeld of the Southern Growth Policies Board, is "outsourcing," a process by which major companies farm out certain basic production tasks to rural towns with cheap labor and rent. To work, outsourcing requires fairly advanced telecommunications.

Fred Williams noted that General Motors is heavily committed to outsourcing. GM now runs several fabrications plants in

Juarez, Mexico, along the Texas border, via an EDS system which controls inventory, production details, etc. The system uses broadband communications from Mexico, and then connects to privately-leased AT&T phone lines, bypassing the local telephone exchange in Texas and Detroit.

As part of its goal of slashing its per-car production costs by $1,000, General Motors also uses telecommunications to order parts and exchange CAD/CAM drawings (engineering and design plans) with suppliers, accelerating the design and production process.

Other examples: Ed Parker told of a commodity news service based in a rural area that could not get daily market quote information because it was tied into a four-party phone line. The problem was solved with a satellite antenna to receive the data.

Ed Parker said that U.S. Forest Service rangers at remote locations are equipped with small transmit-receive stations, so that all stations can report in to headquarters. The Bureau of Land Management has similar but unattended earth stations that transmit data to help fight forest fires.

"Electronic data interchange" (EDI) is a growing trend in many industries, said Richard Adler. Such routine documents as purchase orders, invoices, and bills of lading are now being handled electronically. Roughly 85% of the dollar volume of drugs ordered from drug distributors now occurs through EDI. Burroughs Wellcome will accept orders only through mail or EDI; no phone orders are accepted.

This trend works to the disadvantage of smaller companies which may actually be more efficient, said Adler. One solution has been the Hospital Distributors of America, a consortium of smaller companies which collectively provide electronic, national access to their products via EDI. They constitute a "virtual company," said Adler.

Stuart Rosenfeld added that telecommunications is becoming a new competitive factor in southern states, as manufacturing moves away from low-wage, mass-production activities. More advanced manufacturing requires much closer ties with suppliers and markets, and is more dependent on the movement of information.

Telecommunications
as an Empowerment Tool

A key issue in the emerging role of telecommunications is how it alters—or reinforces—existing power relationships between buyers and sellers. Typically, major corporations use telecommunications to enhance their market advantages, often, if inadvertently, at the expense of rural America, whose use of telecommunications is usually a defensive attempt to stay competitive.

But can telecommunications be used to transform existing market relationships to favor rural America, or at least equalize bargaining power in the marketplace? Several participants expressed great interest in this potential.

One reason this issue is important to rural economies, said Marty Strange, is because "rural economies are characterized by many sellers of undifferentiated products and few buyers—which is the exact opposite of urban markets. This has a special impact on the small commercial farmer, who remains the most omnipresent business activity in rural areas (even if the occupation does not employ the largest number of rural people)," said Strange.

The new trend in many livestock-raising areas is direct buying; the buyer visits larger farms (minimum, 1,000 head of cattle), quotes a price, and makes the buy on the spot. Smaller farmers still have to take their cattle to market, which puts them at a serious bargaining disadvantage. If they think the price quoted upon arrival at market is too low, they do not have any feasible alternatives; maintaining the cattle at market or returning home are both too costly. So they end up being forced to take whatever price is offered.

"What is the potential for telecommunications to remedy this situation so that small farmers can get a price on cattle before moving them to market?" Strange asked. "Packers have scuttled most experiments for telemarketing of cattle because they do not want a more competitive environment. They have monopsonistic power."

Heather Hudson told how one of the major cattle buyers set up a two-way telecommunications system a few years ago so that its buyers-in-the-field, with access to the latest market data, can optimize the price and day of delivery of cattle. The company calculated that if the system allowed them to bid one-half cent lower per pound of meat, the system would pay for itself within six months.

The challenge is to harness this technology to benefit sellers of cattle (farmers) as well. Small entrepreneurs in other businesses that face competitive disadvantages could benefit from this capability, too. An extra fillip, said Hudson, "is that income stays local and helps develop the local economy."

The State of Texas' education agency is taking advantage of this insight, said Fred Williams. It is encouraging school districts to do their own payroll work, accounting, etc., so that instead of paying $25,000 to distant service centers, that money is spent locally and bolsters the local economy.

Rod Bates said that many available telecommunications systems—such as microwave technology owned by public television systems in Nebraska—simply are not being fully exploited in experimental ways. There are a few examples, such as "Agri-vis," which provides the latest market prices for various commodities, and "High-vis" for the hearing impaired. But people often do not have the "comfort level" of innovating with new and unfamiliar technologies.

Telecommunications can bring new vitality to remote, economically isolated communities, said Philip Burgess. He told of a Navajo entrepreneur from a remote region of southeastern Utah who, through a business contact in Japan, built a thriving business exporting his tribe's artwork to Japan, Europe and elsewhere. The business, which employs 150 people, would not be possible without a digital-switched telephone system. Navajos who had left for urban areas are now returning to work for the tribe's business.

Economic Development and Telecommunications

Intuitively, most participants believed that telecommunications is important to rural economic development. But what is actually known, empirically and systematically, about this presumed linkage? Michael Rice asked.

Edwin Parker noted that Andrew Hardy, as part of his doctoral dissertation, documented the historic correlations between telephone availability and economic development. He compiled statistical evidence linking telephones to development, indicating that investment in telephones in one time period correlates with increased wealth in a later period.

Parker added that there is macroeconomic evidence showing that the lower the population density, the greater the economic advantage of having a phone. But what is perhaps most important is the indirect impact of telecommunications in enabling information to be exchanged and used. Railroads themselves did not cause economic development," said Parker. "It was the goods and people transported over the railroad. So it is with telecommunications."

Heather Hudson said that we really do not know exactly how and why telecommunications assists economic development. Still, a number of case studies of Third World rural economies provide useful lessons. These studies were sponsored primarily by the International Telecommunication Union, the World Bank, and the U.S. Agency for International Development.

Hudson urged that we compare studies of Third World nations with U.S. rural economies; learn how to apply plentiful knowledge about the "information sector" to rural economies; and explore secondary uses of information in manufacturing processes.

"We can build a mosaic from existing research," said Hudson, "but we need to build a clearer overview of the national picture." One useful starting point may be Canadian historian Harold Innes' study of the analogy between railroads and telecommunications, she said.

Don Dillman warned that the historic pattern of technology diffusion is for rural areas to lag behind cities. If this happens with telecommunications, first rural areas will not be able to attract businesses; then urban-based businesses will use telecommunications to "suck out" business and capital from rural areas.

Furthermore, said Richard Silkman, universal service—either plain-old-telephone service or enhanced services—may be jeopardized because rural areas will not have the business-related volume usage which, in urban areas, has been and continues to be used to underwrite universal service.

The paradox, said Silkman, is that a fiber optic cable will not be installed for rural areas unless there is an economic justification for it. Yet no economic justification may materialize unless the cable is installed.

Telecommunications may not ensure economic development, but it can provide an infrastructure that enables development to proceed, all factors being equal.

As an example, Silkman cited the city of Portland, Maine. Telecommunications has allowed the city to develop its own financial, legal, accounting and data-processing services, and thereby to serve as an intermediary financial link to rural Maine and northern New England.

The social exchange between mid-sized cities of 60,000-to-200,000 population also "cross-fertilizes" rural areas with new ideas and cultural attitudes, said Cynthia Duncan.

As a first priority, rural areas need to develop local services that substitute for imported services, said Philip Burgess. But for long-term economic development, rural areas must develop a base of traded services. These services will be more stable because they will not be so susceptible to local business cycles.

But it was pointed out that the more significant traded services, such as Omaha's toll-free 800 answering services and Citibank's Sioux Falls credit card operations, are occurring in mid-sized cities, not rural areas.

Michael Rice returned to the original question: Does telecommunications actually spur economic development?

"You can't measure missed opportunities," said Stuart Rosenfeld.

"What you do know," said Philip Burgess, "is that rural America will be left behind, and at a much faster rate, if it does not have better telecommunications. It's harder to make the 'positive case' as convincingly. But you have to take risks," Burgess continued. "That's what leaders are for. Sometimes you make mistakes. But you sometimes have to make a leap of faith."

In short, Michael Rice concluded, enhanced telecommunications may not be a sufficient condition to spur rural economic development, but it is a necessary condition.

Rural Education and Telecommunications

One of the most promising uses of telecommunications in rural America is to improve access to education. "Distance learning" through teleconferencing can provide specialized expertise and training to rural areas that otherwise would not have such educational opportunities.

Distance learning could help close what Scott Howard called "the aspirations gap" in rural America—a culture of low ambition reinforced by the lack of access to telecommunications, information, and education.

What promise does distance learning hold? Besides remedying shortages of specialized expertise in rural areas, telecommunications can help prevent consolidation of school districts, said Marty Strange. "It is important to preserve local participation and local schools."

In the United Kingdom, telecommunications are being used to create "electronic support groups" of affinity groups, such as disabled people, in remote areas, said John Bryden.

In northeastern Minnesota, local education officials and nonprofit leaders built a fiber optic cable between five colleges so that students could take a broader array of courses, via teleconferencing, and obtain four-year degrees. Without this capability, said Jim Roche of the Northspan Group, students would have to travel 400 miles to the Twin Cities.

Philip Burgess said telecommunications has been used in many instances to provide continuing education and professional development. These examples include:

- The LaJolla Western Behavioral Science program has a week-long computer teleconferencing program for high-level corporate executives, held in conjunction with person-to-person meetings.
- The University of Colorado Health Sciences Department has a computer teleconferencing program to train health administrators.

- The Federation of Rocky Mountain States ran an early satellite education demonstration project in the 1970s which had mixed results, but thorough evaluations of the project could prove useful for later experiments.

Stuart Rosenfeld, like most participants, agreed that distance learning may improve the quantity of education in rural areas. But does it really improve the quality of education as well? Too little is known about the effects of distance learning.

While quality of education may sometimes suffer through distance learning, John Bryden insisted that any enhanced access to education is a big improvement for rural residents.

Fred Williams said he is impressed at the new ways being found to increase the personal interactions of distance learning. In the "TI-IN" distance-learning program in Texas, the centralized instructor knows the names of his 30 or so students and there is interactive, point-to-point communication rather than simply mass communication to passive students.

But Rod Bates said that many educators fail to use the technology in ways that truly enhance education. Either there is no interaction between students and teachers, the video is "boring talking heads," or "glitzy production values get in the way of education." As teachers and students become more comfortable with the VCR and other technologies, however, instructional materials are becoming more tailored to user needs.

Don Dillman agreed that many faculty are not trained to use interactive video technologies appropriately; a stand-up lecture is the norm. Bates said that is why it is important that users customize the technology for their particular needs.

New information technologies with larger memory storage are making it easier for users to customize, said Edwin Parker. Using VCRs and CD-ROMs, one can achieve interactivity without teleconferencing.

"But don't all these distance-learning schemes presume a high level of student motivation?" asked Michael Rice. "Does that level of interest exist?"

Hudson agreed. "Motivation is critical. Teleconferencing is less successful for mass instruction. Also, there has to be an institutional setting (such as local tutors or discussion groups) to help provide motivation."

But it works, Hudson stressed. Nurses in rural Texas who want continuing education credits are motivated to learn, even if it is via an interactive audio network. Bates told how insurers are now using teleconferencing to educate their agents about a new insurance investment product.

Burgess agreed that teleconferencing in education is a "highly focused, need-oriented sort of technology." Its chief value, he said, "is getting people into the system who wouldn't get in otherwise." People seeking higher-level education—such as professionals and teachers—may have greater motivation to use these technologies than ordinary students.

But Kenneth Deavers objected that "the people in rural areas who most need to be reached—for basic literacy and skills training, for example—aren't in institutional settings such as schools and workplaces." That's why we must be innovative in devising the institutional settings for reaching rural people, Deavers said.

One solution may be to get people together with their peer groups in their own social milieu, said Mary Mountcastle of MDC, Inc. This can help shy and skittish novices overcome the "comfort factor" problem in using new electronic technologies. That is how farmers in east North Carolina learned to use a computer; they formed a coop and learned together. Perhaps Black churches could be a worthwhile institutional vehicle for learning through teleconferencing.

Richard Adler agreed that "you need a delivery mechanism that involves people." He cited a science teleconferencing project, KidsNet, in which children from geographically diverse classrooms interact with other classrooms and send data from science experiments to a central location. "It is a low-cost way of changing kids' feelings about science education," said Adler. "They feel like they're part of something bigger."

Silkman was skeptical about the potential misuse of distance-learning technologies. "Whenever I hear the word 'teleconferencing' or 'video instruction,' the only justification I ever hear for it is cost. I don't hear about student interest or quality of instruction."

Silkman worried that, given the large capital investments that these technologies require and the very high cost of providing elementary and secondary education, state legislatures will be tempted to promote them as cheap substitutes for "real" teachers and educational materials. Distance learning could end up being used in inappropriate settings, such as grade schools, where it is less effective (and, thus, more expedient) than traditional instructional processes.

3. Strategies for Action

How to Upgrade Rural Telecommunications?

Participants agreed that rural America's limited telecommunications often put it at a disadvantage in today's economy. But what strategies can transform the situation?

This question implies a series of profound changes—in public attitudes toward telecommunications, regulatory policies, configurations of political power, and how to finance such infrastructure investment.

For starters, said Richard Adler, Director of the Teleservices Program for the Institute for the Future in Menlo Park, California, it is a big mistake is "to conceive of telephone service as two phones talking to each other. This misconceives the vast potential of digital telephone networks."

Digital telecommunications allows voice, data, image and graphics to be combined together. They can be compressed, edited, stored and transmitted more efficiently (and thus more cheaply) than existing analog telecommunications systems, which have limited capacity and slower transmission rates.

Digital switching equipment helps greatly reduce the costs of long-distance telecommunications and thus has immense implications for rural economies.

[Andy Roscoe said that 44% of rural communities had digital switching as of 1986. The Northeast will be completely digital by 1992 and Bell South by 1991. Digital upgrades by all independent phone companies could take a generation.]

L.L. Bean runs its immense catalog sales operation from Freeport, Maine (population, 5,000), with digital switching equipment leased from the local telephone exchange carrier. (The switch bypasses the exchange, and so is not available to the average residential phone user.)

Digital switching gives L.L. Bean huge efficiencies, as Scott Howard described: "If I were to increase the average call length by 10 seconds [by using analog equipment instead], the additional cost of the toll-free 800 service alone, not including labor costs, etc., would be over $500,000."

As digital service becomes the norm in urban regions, rural communities are quickly falling behind. But upgrading rural telecommunications quickly runs athwart the question of who will pay for it—and under what terms?

The issue often pits consumer advocates favoring low-cost basic service using existing technologies against businesses favoring advanced telecommunications systems with the costs folded into the rate base paid by everyone.

"We're in the midst of a policy climate," said Michael Rice, "which seeks to allocate actual costs to actual users, without cross-subsidies." The rationale for this trend is to improve efficiencies while financing the upgrading of telecommunications technologies, said Rice.

"If businesses are driven to bypass the local exchanges," said Edwin Parker, "we're going to further disadvantage entrepreneurs in rural areas. Many rural systems need to be upgraded anyway, if only because of the cost of maintaining the existing systems."

"We have got to find a way [for rural areas] to leapfrog up to the latest technologies," said Parker, "rather than simply catch up with existing urban systems."

Richard Silkman of the Maine State Planning Office astutely noted a major roadblock to this goal: public utility commissions generally do not have the statutory authority to consider rural economic development when developing rate structures. That authority belongs with state legislatures.

Yet going to a state legislature to obtain that authority brings to public attention a fact usually obscured by the complexities of the ratemaking process: that ratemaking is a form of income distribution. Three PUC commissioners in Maine allocate $1.2

billion through their rate decisions, said Silkman. Give this power to the state legislature and the ratemaking process immediately becomes politicized.

A chicken-and-egg dilemma complicates the quest for upgraded rural telecommunications. Digital switching technology allows major reductions in costs, but only if a substantial capacity is actually used. As Heather Hudson pointed out, "A 747 plane can provide the lowest cost per mile but only if the seats are full." Yet as the national norms for telecommunications improve, leaving rural towns far behind, "we may need a new definition of 'universal service,'" said Hudson.

Small rural businesses face a special problem in agitating for better telecommunications, said Don Dillman of Washington State University. "In metropolitan areas, they can usually piggyback new services that big users have pioneered. But that doesn't occur in rural areas." Dillman suggested that rural businesses may have to forge some sort of alliance with agricultural concerns to lobby for better telecommunications.

But how can such a major infrastructure investment in telecommunications be justified when the potential benefits are speculative and may never materialize?

That is precisely why the public sector has to become involved, said Martin Strange. That is how electrification came to Nebraska in the 1930s.

"We shouldn't take the political climate as a given," Strange counseled, "because the political climate changes when people take an interest." He added that the current climate is not to eliminate subsidies but merely to privatize them.

Ken Deavers agreed that government has a critical role to play. "One of the past lessons of technology diffusion is that rural regions lag behind urban ones unless public policy deliberately intervenes. Without that intervention, rural will again lag behind—at a time when rural is already under great pressure and undergoing rapid change."

Cynthia Duncan of The Aspen Institute lamented the fact that "people are so slow in recognizing that telecommunications is a public issue. We need to figure out strategies to popularize the issue and open it up to public discussion."

One way to do this, suggested Philip Burgess, is to explain, clearly and simply, what benefits the new technologies can provide. What is happening instead, "lawyers and engineers and policy people who take the political climate as given" are failing to explain and sell the new technologies, Burgess said. What is needed is better leadership to change the policy climate and better marketing savvy to promote the new systems.

What Role Should Government Play?

Breaking the current stalemate in both rural economic development and telecommunications improvements will require active government intervention, most participants agreed.

There are many worthy models to emulate or adapt: the space program, rural electrification, the transcontinental railroads, TVA and Bonneville Power, and other major infrastructure investments.

Kenneth Deavers suggested that the REA, which has largely accomplished its original mission, be rechartered with the mission of modernizing rural telecommunications.

How to do this? Without more interest by the next Administration or Congress, it may be impossible. Still, a logical advocate for revamping the REA would be the National Rural Electric Cooperative Association. While this group is not focused solely on agricultural concerns any more, it does not seem to have the innovative spirit or intellectual capacity to tackle such an ambitious campaign, participants agreed.

What about the "force-fed" technology demonstrations such as "Greenthumb" and "Grassroots"?

They had two major problems, said Hudson. First, the ideas did not originate from the user populations and so were not always useful. Second, the projects were conducted free, so when the funding ran out, they were not ready to stand on their own two feet—and died. Dillman said these projects ought to be tried again now; today's better technologies could make them work.

Projects with social objectives ought to be publicly funded, said Bates. But economic development projects work better with some sort of quasi-public authority with a legislative charter. In Nebraska, the legislature chartered a telecommunications center with a research and development mission. With initial funding of $2 million from the state, the center hopes eventually to be self-supporting, at which point it will pay back the government by selling the government's equity stake in the center.

If economic development is going to work, said Bates, "institutional structures are going to have to adapt. The REA can't adapt fast enough."

In deciding whether to make rural telecommunications investments, the government should not rely solely on cost-benefit analysis, said Stuart Rosenfeld, because it would be entirely too speculative. "We didn't do that for the interstate highways. Besides, the social costs of declining communities aren't part of the cost-benefit equation."

Silkman pointed out that public utility commissions could play a role in telecommunications and economic development, but "we have abrogated responsibility for making them focus on that." For example, when the Maine PUC had a $3 million windfall to dispense—more than the legislature ever spends for economic development—it chose merely to lower residential rates by 50 cents a month.

Michael Rice pointed out the conventional rationale for such a response: market forces, not the heavy hand of government, should shape the course of future investment in telecommunications.

"But that's the worst of both worlds," said Ed Parker, "because this is a regulated environment." Still, replied Rice, billions of dollars in private investment have fueled fiber optics and other telecommunications advances—and regulatory barriers are falling.

"My only point," said Silkman, "is that PUCs are making their decisions with no input from legislatures arguing for rural economic development."

The most important task for government, said Philip Burgess, is to develop institutional mechanisms that aggregate markets. The agricultural extension services created an educated user and delivery system to diffuse technologies. What we want to diffuse are not programs or technologies but ways of aggregating markets.

"So model programs should be institutional experiments that have less to do with technology or rural circumstances than with leadership and empowering people to make demands on the existing system," Burgess said.

Telecottages in America?

One way that Scandinavian governments have spurred the use of telecommunications in rural areas is through telecottages—community centers which provide such services as facsimile and telex transmissions, electronic mail, data processing, language translations, and other services.

The first Swedish telecottage was established in 1985 in Vemdalen, Richard Adler reported. Some 30% of the town's population and all generations now participate in classes and events sponsored by the telecottage. By charging for services to local businesses, the telecottages have reached the break-even point and no longer subsist on government funding. (Some telecottages are run as social services, with no expectation that they will be financially self-supporting.)

The movement has succeeded so well that in September 1988, the 20 Swedish telecottages will open a Stockholm marketing office to solicit business, which will be electronically transmitted to and from the rural towns. Within a few years, another five to ten telecottages are expected to open.

One of the most innovative aspects of the telecottages is their language translation services. Using a network of translators in rural areas, the telecottages collectively offer translation services for a wide range of languages.

Two cultural factors are important to the success of the telecottages, said John Bryden. First, there is the Scandinavian "folk high school" tradition which bolsters the sense of community solidarity. Second, there is a national ethos of decentralization which encourages people to treat the telecottages as town halls or community meeting centers.

Can the telecottage model work in the United States, which puts a greater premium on private-sector solutions? Many telecottage services are already provided by private companies, noted Cynthia Duncan. For example, many photocopy centers have expanded into telecommunications and information services. Ted Bradshaw suggested that the franchise model could provide a vehicle for disseminating these services in the U.S.

Several participants urged that telecottage experiments be tried in the U.S. using public institutions such as libraries, schools, universities, agricultural extension services. Also, county fairs are a traditional forum for exposing people to new things; they could be used to promote telecommunications.

"Telecottages struck me as a practical, modest initiative that, with modifications, could work in the U.S.," said Adler. Different models should be tried and a special emphasis should be put on public outreach.

Future Directions

Given the problems and potential that telecommunications holds for rural economic development, what future directions should be pursued?

The answers fell into two general (and overlapping) categories—research and action. Participants suggested that future research seek to answer the following questions:

1. What criteria and information are needed to develop a long-range strategy for investing in telecommunications in rural areas? [Rosenfeld]
2. Does telecommunications encourage economic growth in rural areas, or does it hasten decline? How does this happen? What are the linkages? [Dillman, Collins, Roche] Case studies would be particularly useful. [Hudson] Studies on the impact on small business would also be helpful. [Williams]
3. What are the factors that attract people to settle in rural areas? [Dillman]
4. How can rural policy allow some degree of community choice while achieving a reasonable pace of implementation? What role should community organizations, and governments at federal, state and local levels, play? [Mountcastle]
5. How can or should policymakers exploit telecommunications to help rural America adapt to change? [Bates]

6. Can a compelling conceptual rationale be developed to promote rural telecommunications as an urgent public issue deserving government attention? [Duncan]

7. How extensive are the technical barriers to installing enhanced telecommunications in rural areas? How many communities do not have digital switches, and what difference might they make? There is a need to build a comprehensive, reliable data base. [Bradshaw]

8. What lessons can U.S. policymakers learn from foreign nations about how new electronic technologies can create jobs, improve native industries, and expand democratic participation? [Bryden]

Participants also suggested several action strategies (which would require further research to implement). These included:

1. *Grassroots Institution-building*

   a. Help build ongoing institutions (user groups, research centers, community centers) that can generate new knowledge about rural telecommunications, advocate their use, and build competence among potential users. [Bollier]

   b. Nurture innovative, decentralized institutions to aggregate markets in rural areas and develop leadership—emulating the model of the agricultural extension service. [Burgess, Silkman]

   c. Forge new types of public/private-sector cooperation to research and implement rural telecommunications initiatives. [Cohen]

2. *Telecommunications Education*

   a. Develop telecommunications education programs for rural entrepreneurs, guided by their indigenous needs. Seminar participants should be charged some fee, even if discounted, so that the program will remain sensitive to market demands. [Roscoe, Silkman]

   b. Develop a rural entrepreneurs' telecommunications support system to provide technical assistance and help meet basic business needs. [Briggs, Jacobson]

    c. Educate rural people about the telecommunications choices they face, so that they can make the best choice for their communities. [Rice]

3. *Mobilize Government.*

    a. Institutionalize a long-term governmental commitment to rural economic development. By adapting the extension service model, the government should foster the use of telecommunications to improve the delivery of human services in rural communities; facilite rural business formation and success; and empower disadvantaged rural people. [Deavers]

    b. Explore political strategies to make this happen. [Sechler]

    c. Revitalize the Rural Electrification Administration to undertake the revamping of rural telecommunications. [Parker]

    d. Educate policymakers, especially at the federal level and at state public utility commissions, about rural telecommunications and economic development. [Holmes]

    e. Develop inspirational anecdotes about telecommunications and rural development successes so that the public, businesses, and government leaders can more easily understand the complex, abstract issues surrounding telecommunications. [Rice]

4. *Telecottages*

    Sponsor a demonstration project of telecottages (after studying in a systematic way the feasibility of creating telecottages in the U.S.). The project should include an evaluation component to assess actual strengths and weaknesses. [Adler, Hudson]

5. *Empowerment*

    Develop applications of telecommunications that will alter existing power relationships, empower the farmer/entrepreneur, and make markets more competitive. [Strange]

If any future conferences such as this one are held, participants recommended inviting officials from the National Rural Economic Cooperative Association, the Rural Electrification Administration, independent telephone companies, congressional subcommittees, long-range planners from regional Bell operating companies (RBOCs), and members of state public utility regulatory commissions.

PARTICIPANTS

Richard Adler, Director, Teleservices Program, Institute for the Future, Menlo Park, California

Rod Bates, Managing General Partner, Bates Video Production, Lincoln, Nebraska

David Bollier, Contributing Editor, *CHANNELS* Magazine, New Haven, Connecticut

Jack Briggs, Executive Director, Macon County Economic Development, Macon, Missouri

John Bryden, Program Director, The Arkleton Trust, Inverness Shire, United Kingdom

Philip M. Burgess, Executive Director, US West, Washington, D.C.

Michael Clark, President, Environmental Policy Institute, Washington, D.C.

Wendy Cohen, Research Fellow, Rural Economic Policy Program, The Aspen Institute, Washington, D.C.

Norman R. Collins, Director, Rural Poverty & Resources Program, The Ford Foundation, New York, New York

Kenneth Deavers, Director, Agricultural & Rural Economy Division, Economic Research Service, U.S. Department of Agriculture, Washington, D.C.

Don A. Dillman, Director, Social & Economic Sciences Research Center, Washington State University, Pullman, Washington

Cynthia Duncan, Associate Director, Rural Economic Policy Program, The Aspen Institute, Durham, New Hampshire

Lynn R. Holmes, Director, Federal Relations, Bellsouth Corporation, Washington, D.C.

Scott Howard, Director, Catalog Operations, L.L. Bean, Freeport, Maine

Heather E. Hudson, Director, Telecommunications Management & Policy Program, McLaren College of Business, University of San Francisco

Andrew Jacobson, Associate Publisher, Telecom Publishing Group, Alexandria, Virginia

Mary Mountcastle, Vice President, Economic Development, MDC, Inc., Chapel Hill, North Carolina

Edwin B. Parker, President, Parker Telecommunications, Gleneden Beach, Oregon

Michael Rice, Director, Program on Communications and Society, The Aspen Institute, Truro, Massachusetts

Jim Rice, Marketing Director, The Northspan Group, Duluth, Minnesota

Andrew Roscoe, Senior Consultant, EMCI Inc., Arlington, Virginia

Stuart Rosenfeld, Deputy Director, Southern Growth Policies Board, Research Triangle Park, North Carolina

Susan Sechler, Director, Rural Economic Policy Program, The Aspen Institute, Washington, D.C.

Richard Silkman, Director, State Planning Office, Augusta, Maine

Marty Strange, Senior Associate, Center for Rural Affairs, Walthill, Nebraska

Frederick Williams, Professor, College of Communications, University of Texas, Austin, Texas

Access charges

Since the divestiture of AT&T, most telephone customers pay access charges, sometimes called subscriber line charges, for access to the public switched network. The charge is theoretically to make up for the subsidies paid by the long-distance companies to the local operating telephone companies. Long-distance carriers pay a different set of carrier access charges to local phone carriers.

ACSN

Appalachian Community Services Network.

AGRICOLA

Database of bibliographical information made available by the U.S. Department of Agriculture (USDA).

AgriData

Agricultural information service provided by AgriData Resources Inc., providing price information, market analysis, research reports, and computer conferencing for special interest groups.

Analog switch

Telephone exchange that switches signals in analog (as opposed to digital) form.

ANI

Automatic Number Identification. Equipment at the telephone company central office recognizes the telephone number of the person making the call, so that information about the call can be sent to the call accounting system or to the called number.

AT&T
American Telephone and Telegraph.

Audio conferencing
Connecting more than two locations into one telephone conversation; often used with special microphones and speakers.

Baud
A unit of transmission speed. Symbols per second.

BETRS
Basic Exchange Telephone Radio Service. A service using radio frequencies to provide rural telephone service.

BOC
Bell Operating Company.

BT
British Telecom.

Cellular telephone service
Mobile telephone system using a series of transmitters in local areas or cells. The call changes frequency as the driver moves between cells. The system allows frequencies to be reused, thus providing much greater capacity than older mobile systems. Calls to and from cellular telephones can be connected into the public switched network.

CFC
National Rural Utilities Cooperative Financing Corporation.

CMN
Computerized Management Network operated by Virginia Polytechnic Institute, offering problem solving for farm management, information retrieval, and electronic mail.

CNN
Cable News Network.

CoBank
National Bank for Cooperatives.

Custom calling services
Special services for telephone customers, e.g., three way calling, call forwarding, and call waiting.

db
Decibel; a measure of signal strength.

dbrnc
A common telephone industry unit for measuring circuit noise.

Digital switch
Computerized telephone exchange that processes voice and data in digital (as opposed to analog) form.

Earth station
The antenna and associated equipment used to receive and / or transmit telecommunications signals via satellite.

Electronic mail
A store and forward service for the transmission of textual messages from a computer terminal or computer system. A message sent from one computer user to another is stored in the recipient's "mailbox" until that person logs into the system. The system then can deliver the message.

EMCI
Economic and Management Consultants International, Inc., Arlington, VA.

Facsimile
Equipment that transmits pages of information over telephone lines and reproduces them at the receiving end.

Fax
See facsimile.

FCC
Federal Communications Commission.

Freeze frame video transmission
The transmission of discrete video picture frames. Freeze frame can be carried on a voice grade telephone line operating at 9600 bits per second.

GAAP
Generally Accepted Accounting Principles.

Gateway

In computer networking, a gateway is the hardware and software used to interconnect different networks, for example two or more Local Area Networks (LANs). In the context of telephone policy, gateway also means the hardware and software used by a telephone company to connect a subscriber to an information provider. Federal Judge Harold Greene, in a recent court ruling in connection with the Modified Final Judgement (MFJ), otherwise known as the AT&T consent decree, has determined that the Regional Bell operating companies are not permitted to offer information services but are allowed to provide gateways to information service providers.

GDP

Gross Domestic Product.

GNP

Gross National Product.

GTE

General Telephone and Electronics.

IBP

Iowa Beef Processors.

Interactive services

Services that enable users to communicate with a computer or with other computer users.

ITU

International Telecommunication Union.

Joint board

Federal State Joint board which is compromised of four state and three FCC commissioners.

LAN

Local Area Network.

LATA

Local Access Transport Area. The geographical boundaries within which Bell operating companies are permitted to carry long-distance traffic.

LEC
Local exchange carrier.

Lifeline
Service fund to help low-income telephone subscribers maintain basic telephone service.

Link Up America
Program to provide federal assistance for one-half the cost of residential installation charges and deposits for telephone service.

LTN
Alaska's Legislative Teleconferencing Network.

MCI
A long-distance telephone company. MCI initially stood for Microwave Communications, Inc.

MFJ
Modified Final Judgement, the AT&T Consent Decree administered by Judge Harold Greene that broke up AT&T.

MHz
Megahertz, one million cycles per second.

Microprocessor
An electronic circuit, usually on a single chip, which performs arithmetic, logic, and control operations, customarily with the assistance of internal memory. The microprocessor is the fabled "computer on a chip," the "brains" behind personal computers and many other electronic devices.

Modem
Acronym for modulator/demodulator. Equipment that converts digital signals to analog signals, and vice versa. Modems are used to send data signals (digital) over the telephone network, which is usually analog.

NARUC
National Association of Regulatory Utility Commissioners.

NASA
National Aeronautics and Space Administration.

NECA
National Exchange Carriers Association.

NRECA
National Rural Electric Cooperative Association.

NRTA
National Rural Telecom Association.

NRTC
National Rural Telecommunications Cooperative.

NTCA
National Telephone Cooperative Association.

NTIA
National Telecommunications and Information Agency (in the U.S. Department of Commerce).

NTU
National Technological University.

NYNEX
Regional Bell operating company serving New York and New England.

ONA
Open Network Architecture.

Online computer services
Information services that are accessible via telephone lines from personal computers and computer terminals.

OPASTCO
The Organization for the Protection and Advancement of Small Telephone Companies.

Party line telephone service
Telephone service which provides for two or more telephones to share the same loop circuit.

Point to multipoint
A circuit in which a single signal goes from one originating point to many destination points.

POTS
Plain Old Telephone Service, basic voice service.

PUC

Public Utility Commission.

RBOC

Regional Bell Operating Company, one of the seven regional holding companies formed as a result of the breakup of AT&T.

REA

Rural Electrification Administration.

RSA

Rural Service Area defined by the FCC.

RTB

Rural Telephone Bank.

RTFC

Rural Telephone Finance Cooperative.

Satellite

A microwave receiver and transmitter in space, usually located in geosynchronous orbit, 22,300 miles above the earth.

SMSA

Standard Metropolitan Statistical Area.

Telecommunications

Any sending or receiving of information as signals or sounds or images by electrical or electronic means.

Teleconference

A conference of three or more people at two or more locations linked by telecommunications. Can involve audio, graphics, computer communications, and/or video.

TI-IN Network

Satellite communications network based in Texas, used to reach rural schools.

TNT

Teleconferencing Network of Texas.

Universal Service

refers to the goal of providing voice telephone service at affordable rates to virtually every household.

USDA

U.S. Department of Agriculture.

USTA

United States Telephone Association.

VHF

Very High Frequency radio signals; the portion of the electromagnetic spectrum with frequencies between 30 and 300 MHz.

Voice mail

A system used to record, store, and retrieve voice messages.

WETN

Wisconsin Educational Telecommunications Network.

Anderson, Leo and Czatdana Inan. "24 Billion Spells Mostly Sunny Skies for the U.S. Telecom Industry." *Telephony*, January 9, 1989.

Bashur, Rashid. "Telemedicine and Health Policy." *Proceedings of the Tenth Annual Policy Research Conference*, ed. Oscar H. Gandy, P. Espinosa, and J.A. Ordover. Norwood, NJ: Ablex, 1983.

Brown, David L. and Kenneth L. Deavers. "Rural Change and the Rural Economic Policy Agenda for the 1980s." In Brown, David L. et al., *Rural Development Research Report 69*, USDA-Economic Research Service, pp. 1–28.

Cleveland, Harlan. 1985. "The Twilight of Hierarchy: Speculations on the Global Information Society." *Public Administration Review*, 45:185.

Deavers, Kenneth. 1988. "Choosing a Rural Policy for the 1980s and 1990s." In Brown, David L. et al., *Rural Economic Development in the 1980s. Rural Development Research Report 69*, USDA—Economic Research Service, pp. 377–395.

Department of Agriculture, Rural Electification Administration. Bulletin Number 300-4, 1984-87.

Department of Agriculture, Rural Electrification Administration. REA Loop Survey, 1986.

Department of Agriculture, Rural Electrification Administration. Statistical Report, Rural Telephone Borrowers, 1984-1987.

Dillman, Don A. In press. "Information Technology in Agriculture: the United States Experience." In *Proceedings of International Conference on Information Technology in Agriculture Food and Rural Development.* Commission of the European Communities. Brussels, Belgium.

Dillman, D.A. and Donald M. Beck. "Information Technologies and Rural Development in the 1990s." *Journal of State Government.* 61(1):29–38, 1988.

Dillman, D.A. "The Social Impacts of Information Technologies in Rural North America." *Rural Sociology* 50:1–26, 1985.

Economic and Management Consultants International, Inc. *The Demand for Cellular Telephone Service in Rural Service Areas,* Second Edition, 1988.

Economic and Management Consultants International, Inc. *The Market for BETR/Cellular/Fixed Rural Radio Telephone Service,* 1987.

Economic Research Service, United States Department of Agriculture. 1988. Unpublished data.

Equatorial Communications Company. *1986 Annual Report.* Mountain View, CA, 1987.

Federal Communications Commission, Industry Analysis Division, Common Carrier Bureau. *Telephone Penetration and Household Characteristics,* 1987.

Fischer, Claude S. "The Revolution in Rural Telephony, 1900–1920." *Journal of Social History,* Fall 1987.

Hardy, Andrew P. "The Role of the Telephone in Economic Development." *Telecommunications Policy,* December 1980.

Hudson, Heather E. *A Bibliography of Telecommunications and Socio-Economic Development.* Norwood, MA: Artech, 1988.

———. "Ending the Tyranny of Distance: The Impact of New Communications Technologies in Rural North America." In *Competing Visions, Complex Realities: Social Aspects of the Information Society,* ed. Jorge R. Schement and Leah Lievrouw. Norwood, NJ: Ablex, 1987.

———. "How Close They Sound: Applications of Telecommunications for Public Participation and Education in Alaska." *Systems, Objectives, Solutions,* November 1982.

———. "Telecommunications and the Developing World." *IEEE Communications Magazine,* Vol. 25, No. 10, October 1987.

———. *When Telephones Reach the Village: The Role of Telecommunications in Rural Development.* Norwood, NJ: Ablex, 1984.

——. and Martin Burch. "Information and the Farm." Center for Research on Communication Technology and Society, College of Communication, University of Texas at Austin, January 1988.

International Telecommunication Union. *Benefits of Telecommunications to the Transportation Sector of Developing Countries*. Geneva: ITU, 1988a.

——. *Contribution of Telecommunications to the Earnings/Savings of Foreign Exchange in Developing Countries*. Geneva: ITU, 1988b.

——. *Information, Telecommunications, and Development*. Geneva: ITU, 1986.

——. *Telecommunications and the National Economy*. Geneva: ITU, 1988c.

National Telecommunications and Information Administration. *Telecom 2000*, NTIA Special Publication 88–21. Washington, D.C. October 1988.

Office of Technology Assessment. *Technology and the American Economic Transition: Choices for the Future*. OTA-TET283. Washington, D.C.: Government Printing Office, 1988.

Parker, Edwin B. *Economic and Social Benefits of the REA Telephone Loan Program*. Geneva: ITU, 1983.

——. "Information Services and Economic Growth." *The Information Society*, Vol. 1, No. 1, 1981.

Pierce, William B. and Nicolas Jequier. *Telecommunications for Development*. Geneva: ITU, 1983.

Pomeranz, Y., Rubenthaler, G., and Sullivan, J. "Are We Ignoring Our Customers?" *Wheat Life*, June 11–12, 1987.

Pool, Ithiel de Sola. *The Social History of the Telephone*. Cambridge, MA: MIT Press, 1984.

Rudd, David. "Regulating the BT Giant: Consultation Without Information," *Telecommunications Policy*, Vol. 12, No. 4, December 1988, pp. 318–322.

Saunders, Robert, Jeremy Warford, and Bjorn Wellenius. *Telecommunications and Economic Development*. Baltimore: Johns Hopkins University Press, 1983.

Stevenson, C.R. "Communication Satellites: A Unique Approach to Remote Base Station Control Links." *Communications*, September 1981.

Walp, Robert A., editor. *Telecommunications in Rural Alaska.* Honolulu: Pacific Telecomunications Council, 1982.

United States Telephone Association. Telephone Statistics, 1984–1987.